# VOLUME FOUR

The Divine Comedy

The Knowledge of the Holy

Pride and Prejudice

The Love of God

# A Taste of the Classics

# VOLUME FOUR

The Divine Comedy

The Knowledge of the Holy

Pride and Prejudice

The Love of God

# A Taste of the Classics

## SUMMARIZED BY KENNETH D. BOA

Biblica™

Biblica Publishing
We welcome your questions and comments.

USA     1820 Jet Stream Drive, Colorado Springs, CO 80921
        www.authenticbooks.com
India   Logos Bhavan, Medchal Road, Jeedimetla Village, Secunderabad
        500 055, A.P.

A Taste of the Classics, Volume Four
ISBN-13: 978-1-93406-813-7

12 11 10 / 6 5 4 3 2 1

Published in 2010 by Biblica

A catalog record for this book is available through the Library of Congress.

Printed in the United States of America

# CONTENTS

# Preface

Christians have a rich heritage of devout saints and brilliant thinkers, many of whom have left us their writings. Those with access to these writings have a treasure trove to help them along their journey of faith.

However, many of us lead frenetic lives that don't leave time for reflection, let alone engagement with some of the best Christian literature from across the generations. Dr. Kenneth Boa has helpfully summarized a number of these classics to give you a taste of what you may be missing. You may find deep refreshment in this book. Or, as with any sampler platter, you may discover a morsel you would delight to savor again. Perhaps you could then pick up the original work with a framework already in place to help you immediately engage the classic. Regardless of how you use this book, we hope your faith will be enriched through the considerable insights of generations before us.

A note on method: Dr. Boa cites numerous passages from each book. Because he proceeds through a book from beginning to end, we have chosen not to cite page numbers. This will create a more pleasant reading experience for you, and you will be able to locate passages from each book by the cues the author gives here.

Since the primary audience for this book is American, we have changed spellings to what is commonly accepted in the United States. However, we have left the original style and capitalization for each author. There are some points where authors used dubious capitalization, but we have chosen not to note them (using [sic]), again for ease of reading. Poetry is usually set in prose, for the sake of space. In this case, the initial capital letter in a line of poetry has been lowercased. The following editions are cited in this book:

Alighieri, Dante. *The Divine Comedy*, 3 volumes. Tr. Dorothy M. Sayers. New York: Penguin Books, 1949, 1955, 1962. Also, *The Divine Comedy*. Tr. Allen Mandelbaum. New York: Knopf, 1995.

Tozer, A. W. *The Knowledge of the Holy*. New York: Harper & Row, 1961.

Austen, Jane. *Pride and Prejudice*. Ed. Donald Gray. New York: W. W. Norton & Company, 1993.

Bernard. *The Love of God*. Ed. James M. Houston. Portland: Multnomah Press, 1983.

Special thanks are due to Cindy Barnwell, who helped Dr. Boa edit and enrich the manuscript for publication.

# The Divine Comedy

## Introduction

Many consider *The Divine Comedy* to be the supreme literary work not only of medieval Christendom but also of all the Christian faith. It *is* a remarkable achievement, perhaps rivaled only by Milton's *Paradise Lost*, which we discussed earlier in this series. I don't know if any poet has ever presented a more compelling vision of the soul's journey toward the love of God than Dante has in his *Commedia*. Only after his death was the word *Divina* added, which seems appropriate since the epic depicts man's hopeless state apart from divine intervention. It is a drama, as I see it, of the soul's choice.

I am relying on two translations as I introduce and examine the text. One of the two is a three-volume edition with translation notes by Dorothy Sayers. Unfortunately, she died before the project was completed, so the last twelve or thirteen cantos were translated by another person. In addition to that text, the Allen Mandelbaum translation, published recently, is very smooth and readable.

The ideal way to read this book, of course, is to start at the beginning and work through all three sections—*Inferno*, *Purgatorio*, and *Paradiso*—observing and learning from Dante's pilgrimage while moving vicariously through the various circles of hell, the ascent of Mount Purgatory, and then ultimately empyrean heaven. Yet I am afraid most readers find themselves bogged down by the complexities of Dante's work almost at once. In fact, it is so filled with allusions to Dante's own life and time that without the knowledge of the historical context, typical readers finds themselves totally lost. Who is he talking about? Who are these people he is addressing? In addition to numerous figures from his own time, Dante also includes many figures from the Bible, the ancient world, and mythology.

He relies a great deal on the Roman poets Ovid and Virgil, even employing Virgil as his guide through hell. Virgil, as we will see, represents the epitome of human reason as well as its limitations. Virgil was widely regarded as the greatest poet of the classical era and held in high esteem by Italians for his epic, *Aeneid*, glorifying the founding of Rome. Essentially, Virgil's epic presented the glory of the Roman Empire, while Dante, inspired by that great work, sought to present the glories of God through the vehicle of the Holy Roman Empire. While Virgil's epic glorified man's achievements, Dante aspired to write an epic whose hero would be God rather than man.

Dante's selection of Virgil as his first guide fits well with his theological and literary purposes. He employs Virgil to convey the limitations of human reason apart from knowledge of truth in God. When Virgil appears in canto II of *Inferno*, the reader learns that he is a resident of that domain, not heaven. He resides in a region identified as Limbo, a place without physical torment, but one of great misery nonetheless.

The inhabitants of that region include virtuous pagans, unbaptized infants, and the unredeemed who predated Christ. They dwell in the reflective and dim light of God's glory, tantalized by their glimpse yet unable to enjoy his presence. The reason for this is symbolic. Most of these individuals sought reason apart from God and mistook it as synonymous with truth. Reason is not the same as truth, however; it merely allows us to perceive revealed truth. It is not a light; it merely dwells in the reflected light of truth. Scripture makes this point clearly when it states, "For God, who said, 'Light shall shine out of darkness,' is the One who has shone in our hearts to give the Light of the knowledge of the glory of God in the face of Christ" (2 Corinthians 4:6).

Virgil then explains he has been assigned by God, via the intercessory pleas of Beatrice (a symbol of divine love), to conduct Dante safely past three beasts and through the bowels of hell. He explains that only by this divinely prescribed route can Dante arrive at Mount Purgatory, his desired destination.

It is theologically significant and fitting that the intervention of Beatrice, the symbol of divine love, permits Dante to seek a relationship with God. Only through God's love, made evident in Christ's incarnation, sacrifice, and resurrection, can man enjoy a relationship with his holy Creator. Later in the epic, revelation and illumination are also personified in additional guides provided to Dante.

Dante masterfully interweaves theological, political, and mythological elements with astronomy, geometry, and chronology—a massive amount of knowledge—in a way that is convincing and powerful. Furthermore, his epic relates intimate personal experiences, and few writers have ever displayed their own strengths and weaknesses as unreservedly as Dante or interpreted the universe so consistently in terms of their own soul's aspiration.

## Allegorical Structure

Understanding Dante's allegorical structure becomes the key to proper appreciation of this work. He offers an allegorical picture of the soul's movement either toward God or away from him. A common problem when people try to tackle Dante's work, however, is that they tend to focus on just the first volume, if they even read all of that. Many readers get all wrapped up in the graphic squalors of the inferno—all the gore and gruesomeness. The problem with this casual approach to the poem is that it is almost like spending a few days visiting a great city and then judging that city solely by touring its cellars and sewers. The reader who stops after reading *Inferno* misses the central point of Dante's great allegory: God has intervened in the hopeless lives of mankind via Christ's incarnation, death, and resurrection. Inferno is the inevitability man faces apart from redemption through Christ; empyrean heaven is the hope and certainty of the redeemed.

*The Divine Comedy*, as we will see, chronicles a journey upward; it functions as an extended metaphor not only of the afterlife, but also of the earthly quest for meaning and truth. Through his characterization, Dante explores the wilderness of his own soul and depicts the opposition it faces, from both within and without. It is really an internal journey communicated through an extended allegory.

Yet Dante's allegorical structure contrasts greatly with most familiar allegories, such as John Bunyan's later work. Dante chooses not to personify abstractions overtly but rather to bring to life fictional and historical characters who characterize the impediments that divide man from God. He frames these individuals within the eternal consequences of their sin natures and choices. Thus, the literal meaning of this story is the least important part of it. To read it only at face value is to miss much of its vibrant power.

## Theme

I would like to suggest that the theme of this book, the unified theme, is *amore*, or love—not man's but God's. Dante's work depicts the misery and diminishment of the soul when it exists without love, and he then contrasts that existence with the joy that love affords. He illustrates that the real quest of life involves coming into relationship with the One for whom the soul was actually created. Dante himself put it this way: "I want to demonstrate truths that no one else has dared to attempt." Many will agree that he accomplished this lofty goal.

He was well aware that this was virtually a transcendent

kind of work and intended that it be his life's defining statement. Indeed, he was aware of that both theologically and aesthetically. His objective was the creation of something new, an inimitable work that would span the depths and the horrors of hell, the climbs of purgatory, and finally attain to the heights of heaven and the presence of the living God.

Dante combined both Scholasticism and mysticism, both the academic and the contemplative. He integrated ancient thought—antiquity—with medieval Christianity, and his work actually served to bridge the gap between the Middle Ages and the Renaissance.

## Dante's Life

Dante Alighieri was born in 1265 and lived until 1321, right on that cusp of the medieval synthesis with the Renaissance. In fact, he had a good deal to do with that synthesis. He was able to unite a kind of sacred concept of empire with the spiritual concept of the church, implying that the two could coexist in a way that had not been seen before. His work offered a synthesis of the courtly world and the very different world of Scholastic wisdom.

At this point, I would like to interject a word about Dante's own life and his writings. He was born in Florence, Italy, and belonged to a noble but somewhat impoverished family. He followed a basic course of education and probably attended the university at Bologna, receiving the typical kind of education offered at that time. The academic *trivium* (the word from which we get the word *trivia*) included grammar, logic, and rhetoric. He went beyond that and also studied the more advanced *quadrivium*, which, as its name suggests, represents the next four levels: arithmetic, music, geometry, and astronomy. Theology was not taught as an isolated subject because everything was connected into a theological construct in such a way that theology, the queen of the sciences, was the unifying vision among the seven academic disciplines. Dante evidently became a master of these studies.

He also studied poetry and painting. He became proficient in these arts and seems to have possessed a comprehensive knowledge of virtually everything. In fact, he started work on a book called *Convivia*, which means "banquet." It was intended to be an encyclopedia of all knowledge. Although he died before he could complete it, just the undertaking of such an endeavor indicates the wealth of the knowledge he must have possessed. His impressive intellect is evident in the knowledge beautifully illustrated in this work.

I'd like to mention one particularly significant moment in Dante's early life. When he was about nine years old, his father took him to a May Day party, and there he met the host's daughter, Bice di Folco Portinari, the "Beatrice" of *The Divine Comedy*. She was about a year younger than Dante, and this meeting virtually changed his life. It was love at first sight, but not the kind of love one would ordinarily expect of a young boy; it was love that impassioned and inflamed his soul. He described the experience by saying, "Behold, a god stronger than I has come to build and rule over me." His life was never the same. Some years later, when he was eighteen, he caught sight of Beatrice again, and she was like a revelation to him, with her smile, beauty, and ineffable courtesy. She acknowledged him and spoke to him by name in the street. It was the only time she spoke to him, however, because the next time they met, some scandalous rumors about him forced her to refuse his salutation. He learned, at that point, that love could be an initiation into suffering as well as to ecstasy, something we have all learned ourselves, in one way or another.

The point I want to stress is that this particular vision of love became something far more significant to Dante than mere puppy love or some kind of romantic experience. Dante and Beatrice had no personal romantic relationship. In fact, Dante married another woman, and Beatrice died at the age of twenty-four. Yet throughout his life, she served as the inspiration and ideal of divine love. Our present culture has a way of reducing everything to the lowest common denominator and viewing most experiences through a sexual orientation, and it is therefore difficult to grasp the kind of image of courtly love that existed in the Middle Ages. It is important for us to recognize that Dante's idealized love for Beatrice had a bearing on his life and literature and served to point him to a vision of an even greater love.

For a period, though, he allowed himself to be seduced by the "lady philosophies," and in this sense he pursued other lovers. The literary Beatrice, when she meets him in *Purgatorio*, chides him for having abandoned his original love—his vision of grace—and questing instead after human reason and philosophy. With regard to Beatrice, Dante was not unlike Boethius, who, in the *Consolation of Philosophy*, personified philosophy as a woman, "Sophia."

For a period of time Dante appeared to be missing his true calling by falling in love with human reason. He married

Gemma di Manetto Donati when he was only about twenty years old, and they had five children. For several years his life was filled with preoccupations and instability. He made the mistake, I think, of becoming consumed with politics and ambition and lost his focus for a while in the process.

All three canticles of *The Divine Comedy* contain allusions to the political turmoil in Florence during Dante's time. Italy was composed of a series of city-states, and there were numerous territorial struggles between them, as well as between the papacy and bishops. In addition, there were ongoing guild wars. It was quite a mess.

A major division in Florence resulted from a rift between its two major political parties, the Guelfi and the Ghibellini. The Guelfs were more interested in a spiritual kind of authority, and Dante sided with them and became a leader. When the Guelfs went out of favor in 1302, he was exiled from Florence. Under Pope Boniface VIII, Dante had been sentenced to death on a trumped-up charge, and only exile preserved his life. Dante regarded Boniface as corrupt and held him in contempt. In fact, he assigned this pope to a particularly ignoble level in his hell.

On a side note, some readers have criticized Dante for being nasty to people he didn't like by assigning them to various levels of his *Inferno*, thinking him rather uncharitable to place his friends in heaven and his enemies in hell. Yet his characterization choices are not that simple; they also function as symbols and images. They are not to be interpreted in a merely literal way but within the framework of his allegorical narrative. So I think that such criticisms are not entirely fair.

We must return to Dante's personal situation, however. As a result of the split between Florence's two major political factions, he was subjected to twenty years of exile, from 1302 until his death in 1321. He never returned to Florence, even when his increasing fame led to an invitation to return. It was conditional, however, and as a matter of pride, he chose to remain in solitary exile. Even his wife did not join him, and it was many years later, when he finally stopped roaming and settled down, that his children joined him. During those lonely years, it is believed that he traveled perhaps as far as Paris and may have studied at the university there. Other stories of that period suggest he might even have gone as far as Oxford, though there is no evidence to suggest that he did.

In any event, he studied and wrote despite the chaos in his personal life, creating this great work and several others. He likely started on *The Divine Comedy* some time around 1308 and finished it shortly before his death. He was stripped bare during this period of his life. He lost his love, his youth, his earthly goods and family, and even his citizenship. Additionally, he lost the possibility of active political usefulness, something he wanted very badly. Nevertheless, he joined the Guild of Doctors and the Apothecary Guild. By the way, in Dante's day, books were sold in apothecary shops, so it makes sense that a writer would be affiliated with that guild.

From the vantage point of a political exile, Dante observed the corruption of the church, and much of *The Divine Comedy* criticizes this corruption and reveals Dante's longing for the time when the world would be brought under the authority of God once again. There was one man, Henry VII, whom Dante hoped would fill that role as peacemaker within the Holy Roman Empire, but Henry died in 1313. Yet in *The Divine Comedy*, Dante describes him as a possible temporal savior of the world, hoping somehow that Rome would be the place that God would establish a just reign in a secular realm. Dante's ideal government was not one merely under the authority of the pope; he desired two separate authorities, one led by God and one authorized by God—one to provide the spiritual guidance, another to provide the secular.

In his latter years Dante worked in Verona and Ravenna. He acquired a patron in Ravenna who finally afforded him enough stability to allow some of his children to join him as he continued to work. At one point, he was sent as an emissary to Venice; on his return he traveled through a swampy area and contracted a disease. He died shortly after his return to Ravenna. There is an account that following his death his children and friends could not find the final thirteen cantos of *The Divine Comedy*. Supposedly, someone dreamed that they would be found in a musty area in a former house, and, as the story goes, that is where the remaining cantos were recovered. The literary world would have been greatly impoverished, in my view, had these vital sections been lost, for this work becomes more poetically exquisite as it progresses in the celestial vision.

## Style and Structure

Next we need to explore the style of *The Divine Comedy* and some of its architectural and structural highlights. Because of its complexity, I will hardly have space to scratch the surface. My own study of this book has made me realize that I really want to teach a course on the entire work, as it would actually be a delight to walk readers through it thoroughly and study the incredible literary, historical, philosophical, theological, and cosmological images represented in the work. As it is, in this context there is only room to provide a structural sketch or overview.

The poem follows an intricate and Trinitarian structure. In fact, Dante invented a metrical structure to fit his theological purpose: the *terza rima* pattern. His poem contains one hundred cantos, each composed of three-line stanzas called *terzains*, or tercets. Each tercet contains thirty-three syllables and boasts an interlocking end-rhyme pattern of aba / bcb / cdc, and so on. The brilliance of this poetic structure becomes evident when the reader understands how this deliberate pattern contributes to Dante's structural terrain.

Beginning with *Inferno*, this poetic spiral of interlocking rhyme leads the reader along the descent to central hell. Later in the epic, after a cosmological inversion, which we will discuss later, the pattern spirals upward as the pilgrim Dante ascends first Mount Purgatory and then empyrean heaven. Dante scholar John Freccero attributed even more significance to the pattern as a theological element, asserting that the interlocking pattern propels the motion of the poem in a forward progression.

This interpretation works on multiple levels. First, Dante is a pilgrim, progressing through three unearthly domains. Second, the poem encompasses two types of movement: descent and ascent. Both are portrayed as irresistible forces.

The downward pull of sin, metaphorically depicted by Dante as a gravitational force, pulls the sinner toward eternal death. The upward pull of grace, depicted as levity, pulls the purgated pilgrim toward eternal life.

The movement of the terza rima structure works ideally to illustrate both theological truths. Sin inevitably leads to death; God's grace alone reverses that downward pull as he draws man to himself and joy. Early church scholars used a passage in Ephesians to support this theory, which they termed *recapitulation*. Ephesians 1:10 and Galatians 4:4 describe Christ's incarnation as occurring in "the fullness of the time." Biblically, all of human history fits into three divisions: (1) "In the beginning was the Word," (2) the promise of the Seed and Redeemer, and (3) Christ's incarnation and fulfillment of that promised redemption. Dante includes this theological interpretation in his work through his structure. The recapitulation, or reestablishment of what was in the beginning, becomes possible only through Christ's incarnation and resurrection, making, in this view, history the movement both away from the Word and back to the Word. Dante's structure reminds the reader that salvation exists in three time zones, so to speak. It is historical in the promise of a coming Savior, the incarnation, and the resurrection; it is present in the fact of the availability of salvation; it is future in its ultimate fulfillment in the promised return of Christ and the glorification of the true saints. In this aspect and many others, Dante relied heavily upon Augustinian theology and style, and according to Augustine time is merely God's poem: an account of the death of the fall (and death) through the incarnation of the Word.

The larger poem is divided evenly into three canticles: *Inferno*, hell; *Purgatorio*, purgatory; and *Paradiso*, heaven. Each of these divisions contains thirty-three cantos (chapters), structured in the terza rima pattern. You will notice that this then adds up to only ninety-nine cantos. There is an additional canto, an introduction, that establishes Dante's context and purpose at the beginning of *The Divine Comedy*; and when it is included, the number of cantos totals one hundred, a symbolically significant number.

Numbers were very important in the medieval world, and the structure of Dante's poem symbolizes unity and completeness. The reoccurrence of the number three alludes to the Trinity. The number four serves as a symbol of man, and the number seven symbolizes perfection, completion, and unity. Finally, in a medieval culture fascinated with numerology, the number ten held a special significance. It was regarded as symbolic of God's omnipresence. Dante's decision to fit his poem into one hundred cantos was therefore no accident; one hundred is the square of ten, fitting perfectly into his structural scheme. Additionally, each domain in Dante's cosmology is composed of ten primary levels.

He also used a metrical pattern called the *hendecasyllable*. It is a line of eleven syllables with five accentual beats, adding up to thirty-three syllables per tercet. So, he created a complex poetic structure that in Italian scans perfectly but is nearly impossible to translate effectively. Some people have actually learned Italian just to read this great work in its original language. I haven't done that yet, but curiosity has tempted me to make the effort. I imagine it would be something akin to my experience in seminary. Seminary requirements forced me to learn Greek and Hebrew, and I must say that reading the Bible in its original languages is like the difference between viewing color images and black-and-white ones. You get the images all right, but you miss the nuances. The same is true of translations; you get the sense of the meaning but miss so much from the original. Yet whether read in the original or via a translation, there is a grandeur in this book. Dante has been described as "the most piercing intellect ever granted to the sons of men," and he is a poet who walks as an equal among Homer, Aeschylus, Virgil, and Shakespeare.

The entire poem deliberately suggests the architecture of a medieval cathedral, with *Inferno* symbolizing the crypts beneath the church and lower portion of the structure; then *Purgatorio* is represented by the sanctuary building and ascending multiple spires characteristic of many cathedrals; and finally, *Paradiso* is represented in the central and highest spire of the grand cathedrals, which points man toward God. The astronomical structure of Dante's universe is, of course, Ptolemaic, reflecting the geocentric concept of the universe promoted by the papacy and church at that time.

## Overview of *Inferno*

Dante places himself as the thirty-five-year-old pilgrim/tourist of his poem, symbolizing the midway point in his life and alluding to Psalm 90:10–12, which states, "As for the days of our life, they contain seventy years, or if due to strength, eighty years, yet their pride is but labor and sorrow; for soon it is gone and we fly away. Who understands the power of Your anger and Your fury, according to the fear that is due You? So teach us to number our days, that we may present to You a heart of wisdom." Dante's guided journey through the terrors of hell and purgatory and his subsequent glimpse of heaven teach him his need for salvation, as well as his need to "number [his] days." He describes this at the very beginning of the first canto:

> When I journeyed half of our life's way, I
> found myself within the shadowed forest, for
> I had lost the path that does not stray. Ah, it is
> hard to speak of what it was, that savage forest,
> dense and difficult, which even in recall renews
> my fear, so bitter death is hardly more severe.
> I cannot clearly say how I entered the wood, I
> was full of sleep just at the point where I had
> abandoned the path. (*Inferno*, canto I)

He grasps that his soul is in peril because he has abandoned the path that leads to God and is heading in the wrong direction. He is then given this vision of hell so that he can be capable of transferring his affections to those true goods for which the heart was made.

Early in the poem, he attributes his salvation to three symbolic intercessors: Beatrice, symbol of divine love; Lucia, symbol of divine light (illumination or revelation); and Rachel, symbol of the contemplative, meditative, or spiritual life. Prior to the first divine intervention, Dante is pursued by the Leopard of Malice and Fraud, the Lion of Violence and Ambition, and the She-wolf of Incontinence (sins resulting from a lack of self-control). Some critics have theorized that the beasts represent particular categories of sin that plague man in his various stages/ages of life from youth to old age. Lust often preys on the youthful man, ambition and violence typically mark the adult man in his quest for power, and malice and fraud are symptomatic of the aging person, for whom acquisition and greed (materialism) become problematic.

Dante's descent into hell strategically begins on Good Friday, and he emerges from hell at sunrise on Easter morning, symbolizing his newfound hope in a resurrected Christ. The remainder of his pilgrimage takes place during the week following Easter. Like all classical epics, Dante's work emphasizes an underworld, or netherworld, visitation, but his is clearly for the purpose of showing the limitations of man's reason and efforts. The inscription over the gate of hell makes this very clear:

> I am the way into the city of woe.
> I am the way to a forsaken people.
> I am the way into eternal sorrow.
> Sacred justice moved my architect.
> I was raised here by divine omnipotence,
> primordial love and ultimate intellect.
> Only those elements time cannot wear
> were made before me, and beyond time I stand.
> Abandon all hope ye who enter here. (*Inferno*,
> canto III)

Very obviously, Dante alludes to the words of Christ in John 14:6: "I am the way, and the truth, and the life; no one comes to the Father but through Me."

Here Dante parodies Christ's declarative statements of

hope. While Christ is the way to salvation, the horror of independence from God results in residence in the city of woe (likely an allusion to Augustine's "city of man"), which is populated by a forsaken and sorrowful people. Christ is also the truth, and hell is an eternal reminder that truth is not relative. Regardless of man's response to or rejection of it, truth itself remains unchanged. Sacred justice motivated God to design hell, for he respects the wills of those who chose something other than him. In a terrifying paradox, Dante asserts that hell was also motivated by primordial love and ultimate intellect. In other words, love and justice made hell necessary. When man comes to the end of earthly things, there must be an option for those who still insist on having their own wills gratified, and that option—tragically—necessitates hell. Dante's gate reminds the reader that man's will still enables him to live apart from God and that when that choice is honored by God, all hope must be abandoned.

God's primary attributes are love, light, and life; and hell is the complete absence of those attributes. It is the epitome of hate and despair, darkness and death. Just as God's priceless gift of salvation is eternal, so, too, is the fulfillment of man's will when he rejects God's gift. As the inscription states, hell stands beyond time. This is the horror of Dante's hell and the sobering realization of the pilgrim Dante as he enters the gate to inferno.

From the gate, he moves into the vestibule, a place where the opportunistic are punished. Here are those individuals who refused to take sides or positions in life; they focused only on self-preservation and self-gratification. Now terrible winds whip these sinners about as they futilely chase after elusive, unidentified banners. Since in life they followed no leader but their own inclinations, in death they are blown about erratically against their wills.

Next Dante and Virgil encounter Limbo, the place reserved for the virtuous pagans and unbaptized innocents. Here, as mentioned earlier, the residents dwell in the dim, reflective light of heaven. This is the only level of hell that has light, and its presence is symbolic. In life, these virtuous individuals sought truth through reason, misunderstanding that reason and rational thought were given to propel man to seek God. The reflected light indicates the value of human reason yet also reminds the reader of its inadequacy.

After Limbo, Dante makes a point of noting that the residents live in utter darkness, confusion, and alienation. Ten levels make up Dante's hell, and those are divided into two central categories: sins of impulse and sins of volition. Circles I–V house those sinners whose lusts, impulses, and instincts led them to destruction. Dante uses common terms of his day to describe such sins: *concupiscence* and *incontinence*. Concupiscence derives from the name of the Roman god of love, Cupid, and implies impulsive sins of a lustful or sexual nature. Incontinence derives from a word meaning to lack control, for a lack of self-control typically leads to sin.

Dante assigns the upper-hell residents to the following levels: Circle I, Limbo; Circle II, the Carnal; Circle III, the Gluttons; Circle IV, the Hoarders and Wasters; Circle V, the Wrathful and Sullen. Each circle is characterized by an appropriate terrain, setting, and punishments. For instance, the Gluttons are immersed in a stinking, swamplike garbage dump. This is fitting because all they produced in life was garbage, due to their self-indulgence, so now they have themselves become eternal refuse.

Dante's upper and lower regions of hell are distinguished by a clearly demarcated boundary. Lower hell is encased within the walled city of Dis. Here Dante once again borrows from Greek and Roman mythology, where Dis was the god of the underworld and the dead. Dante's Dis, however, is a parody of a great city. Its walls and towers are red, the unnamed tower that stands nearby is a minaret, and its architecture is clearly reminiscent of the Muslim world. Dante employs this imagery for two purposes, one historical and the other theological. First, Islam was the enemy of the Holy Roman Empire; second, Muslims rejected Christ and therefore his offer of redemption. This is something they share with all of the residents of lower hell, where Dante confines those who sinned volitionally or deliberately.

Ironically, the city of Dis is no great, fortified city. Upon closer inspection, it is evident that its towers and fortifications are actually chimneys, and once within its walls, no residents are visible—only heard. Its function is not to withstand invasion but to prevent escape; it is a prison and graveyard. Smoke bellows from its towers/chimneys while the screaming souls of the damned burn within its boundaries, encased in fiery tombs.

Within Dis's walls are the five lower levels of hell: Circle VI, the Heretics; Circle VII, the Violent; Circle VIII, the Fraudulent and Malicious; Circle IX, the Traitorous; Circle X, Satan and three significant traitors. As in upper hell, the settings and punishments are tailored to the sins. Particularly important to note are the sinners' unrepentant attitudes all through hell. Having rejected God, they are incapable of pity or remorse and are characterized only by fear, hate, and anger. Their corrupt wills still reign supreme, and they are sorry only for their misery, not for their crimes.

One of the interesting aspects of Dante's lower-hell symbolism involves the *bolgias* of Circle VIII. This particular area is subdivided into ten circles, each of which contains a particular category of fraud or malice. In Italian, *bolgia* connotes three potential interpretations: "ditch or bog," "pocket," "offering bag." All three connotations work beautifully with Dante's thematic purpose at this level.

Circle VIII is the home of many religious figures, not pagans in the traditional sense of the word but Catholic leaders. Dante uses this circle in particular to criticize the corruption that had infested the medieval church, and the subdivided sins of this level reinforce the extent of that corruption. The ditches symbolize the schisms and factions that thwarted church unity and effectiveness. Their pocketlike quality alludes to the money embezzled and pocketed by so many officials within the church, as well as the fact that many churchmen were metaphorically "in the pockets" of the rich and powerful. Finally, these *bolgias* are also symbolic of the type of offering purse or bag used in the Middle Ages: a deep, lined bag attached to two wooden handles. Just as these churchmen had defiled their offices by misappropriating God's money, in Dante's hell they are now housed and tormented in metaphorical offering bags. Throughout hell, Dante employs parodies of Christian symbolism to illustrate the depravity of the sins he highlights.

The symbolism of Circles IX and X is the most impressive

and important of *Inferno*, for it is here that Dante's central theological theme becomes apparent. As the pilgrim Dante progresses toward central hell, the approach is marked by what appears to be, from a distance, a fortress topped by guard towers. Upon closer inspection, it is seen for what it is really is—a ridge of ice in which the Giants of classical mythology are imprisoned and posted as mock guards. Dante's image alludes to an actual Italian fortress that measured a half kilometer in circumference and boasted fourteen towers. Here in hell he mocks the idea of a fortress as security, an allusion to the many Old Testament verses warning that the fortresses in which the evil place their trust provide no protection from God's wrath.

Within the circle of Giants is the first ring of the central pit, Caina, named for the biblical Cain and representative of those who behave treacherously against kin (family). Next is Antenora, named for the classical Antenorus, who betrayed his countrymen. The third ring contains those who have committed treachery against guests, namely offenders of the classical code of hospitality. Here resides Ptolomea (not the astronomer), who murdered his father-in-law at a feast. He is surrounded by others who also defied the ancient code. The final circle is Judecca, named for the biblical Judas. Here reside those who committed treachery against their masters. It is significant that the most treacherous of this category is Satan himself, who in futility led the angel rebellion that ushered disorder into God's universe.

Satan's plight is perhaps a bit surprising to readers, for instead of proverbial fire and brimstone, Dante's central pit is a place of darkness, death, and ice. This, however, is fitting in light of God's absence from hell, for without him, there is no light and therefore no heat. Here the damned are frozen in various positions and states of decomposition. Satan is blackened by frostbite and in a perpetual state of decay. Dante uses the decay imagery to remind the reader of the state of the body and soul apart from God's redemptive work. Satan is ironically embedded in ice up to his hips; however, his imprisonment is an act of his own will. Dante's Satan perpetually beats his batlike wings in an effort to free himself, and yet his efforts only serve to freeze all the waters of Cocytus into a vast glacial prison.

Here Dante very clearly suggests that the nature of sin is the misuse of reason and the will. Man's efforts to achieve his own will in rejection of God's will only subjugates him to misery, yet like Satan, he foolishly hopes that his futile actions can result in something useful or gratifying.

Satan is presented as a grotesque parody of the triune God. Dante relies on a variety of complicated images and allusions to clarify and add significance to the parody. First, Satan lacks the distinct personas of the Trinity; he is merely a beast-demon amalgam with three faces. He possesses no sovereignty, omniscience, or omnipresence. He exercises no power over his domain or the residents within his domain. In contrast to the Trinity, he is not characterized by fellowship, unity, or creativity. As Lucifer was formerly beautiful, so Satan is hideous. His body suggests animal and demonic characteristics, and his three distorted faces mar his once perfect image. He is mute, for he is condemned to eternally chew the other three traitors of central hell: Brutus and Cassius, conspirators against Caesar, and Judas, betrayer of Christ. Even the choice of these individuals fits perfectly within Dante's literary and theological purpose. Since he is emulating facets of Virgil's great classical epic, he selects the two men he deems the worst traitors of the Roman Empire. Since he aspires to write a new type of epic, a Christian poem, he selects Judas as the supreme traitor of Christendom.

Dante also incorporates significant color imagery in his depiction of Satan. His body is dark, black, and rotting. His faces are tricolored: brownish black, yellowish white, and fiery red. These color choices correspond well with early church tradition concerning the symbolism of the mulberry bush. There was a famous classical myth about two lovers named Pryamis and Thisbe. According to the myth, Pryamis mistakenly believed that Thisbe had died, and so he killed himself. When Thisbe, who had not died, found her dead love, she too killed herself. Their blood supposedly spattered the white berries of a nearby mulberry bush, and forever after the berries were red in memoriam of their love. Early church theologians Ambrose and Augustine appropriated the classical mulberry symbol to depict and teach Christian concepts. They based their interpretations on Luke 17:6, which states, "And the Lord said, 'If you had faith like a mustard seed, you would say to this mulberry tree, "Be uprooted and be planted in the sea"; and it would obey you.'" Both men noted the unique trait of the mulberry: when its fruit is young, it appears white; as it matures, the fruit turns red; when it overripens, the berries blacken. Abrose explained that the white symbolized Satan's original state, the red his quest for power, and the black the decay his rebellion produced. St. Augustine's interpretation was slightly different. He argued that the tree represents the gospel of Christ and the cross. He also noted that the berries are not pure white but waxen or off-white, symbolizing man's fall from his pristine prefall state. He used the red of the mature berries to symbolize Christ's wounds as he hung on the tree/cross and the black of the rotting berries to represent the black sins for which Christ died.

The significance of these colors then applied to Satan is that they depict his damnation and repurpose him as a reminder of the cross. Fixed as he is in the ice, with outstretched arms and wings, he suggests a crucifixion pose. Furthermore, as the men approach the creature, Virgil explains that they must scale Satan's torso, hip, and leg as they pass out of the central pit. This crucifixion parody serves as a means to pass through central hell into another dimension.

At this point, the men begin what appears to be another descent along Satan's hip, but as they emerge from the opening alongside his thigh, they find themselves in a sunlit and reverse pole, viewing Satan's legs as they extend upward into the air. While they were in hell, the universe appeared to be right side up. Now that they are nearing the base of Mount Purgatory, however, they are able to see sin and damnation for what they have always been, an inversion of goodness and life.

Satan, upon his eviction from heaven, was thrown down into the pit, and there he has remained, fixed upside down in ice and dirt. The polarity change that occurs here at the exit from hell is of particular importance. Sin had metaphorically turned the world upside down; it had inverted the universe and distorted man's perceptions. Now, Dante sees Satan for what he really is, from God's perspective. Charles Williams thought, and I think he is probably right, that Dante's depiction of Satan's plight is among his greatest images. "Dante," says Williams, "scatters phrases on the difference of the place. It is treachery but it is also cruelty. The traitor is cruel. What you have is a cold and cruel egotism, where Satan is seen as being completely immobile, frozen into immobility and that is the final state of sin where it cannot make choices anymore."

Having crossed the zero point of polarity, Dante and Virgil then pass from gravity into levity. As mentioned earlier, gravity symbolizes man's sin nature that pulls him irresistibly toward damnation, while levity represents God's grace and love that similarly draw man to himself.

Critic John Freccero elaborates on this imagery by suggesting that Satan's raised arms also relate to the Platonic cosmic dimensions of up, down, left, and right. He goes on to explain that "education consists of righting the inverted world and distinguishing right from left; such a conversion, however, is accomplished on the cross of Christ" (*Dante, the Poetics of Converion*, p. 183). Long before Dante, Plato had suggested that the disease of man is his inability to properly recognize up from down and left from right in the moral sense. To quote Frecerro, "The disorder of the soul is represented in the *Divine Comedy* by the soul's disorientation" (p. 183). Jesus Christ becomes the Great Physician, the only one able to correct man's metaphoric state of vertigo.

## Topography and Structures of *Inferno*

There is much significance in the topographical and structural features of Dante's hell. The narrowing, downward spiral has already been mentioned, but it is characterized by cliffs, swamps, burning plains, rivers of boiling blood, impassible rock slides, and fields of ice. Four significant rivers flow through hell, and all are borrowed from mythology. Acheron serves as the boundary between the vestibule of hell and the first circle. Its location just before Limbo reveals its purpose: it is a symbol of remorse. Only in Limbo are the residents remorseful; in every other circle, they are merely angry or afraid.

The river Styx divides upper and lower hell and forms sort of a moat around the city of Dis. It symbolizes hate. Dante assigns it a very similar role to the one it played in Greek mythology, where it separated the land of the living from the domain of the dead. Phlegethon, a river of fire, is located at the entrance of Circle VII. The fire symbolizes anger, and all of the lower-hell residents are characterized by this emotion. In mythology, fire supposedly released the soul to its rest, but here, the fire merely torments. The final river in *Inferno* is Cocytus, a symbol of misery, sadness, and tears. In fact, Dante explains that the tears of the damned contribute to this river, causing a flood that freezes into the frozen lake that imprisons Satan and the traitors. It is significant that it is at Cocytus that the pilgrim Dante grasps the necessity of the cross and Christ for salvation, and he weeps with gratitude as he passes out of the central pit into the dawn of Easter morning.

The intrinsic role of Dante's first canticle within the context of the entire epic must not be minimized. Hell is the epitome of hate, despair, darkness, and death. Shakespeare's Hamlet pondered what was "this quintessence of man." In other words, he asked what distinguished man from everything else in the created universe. The answer is plain. God made man is his own image, with the ability to exercise his will in rebellion to God's. Yet God created man's will to operate ideally only when submitted first to him. Sinful man perpetually asserts his autonomy and independence. That is sin. The ultimate assertion of autonomy is damnation—separation from the Creator. It is the horror of Dante's hell and infinitely more. This is the sobering realization of Dante as he exits hell into new life.

## Introduction to *Purgatorio*

We now turn to the second of the three canticles, *Purgatorio*. As we discussed *Inferno*, we saw that Dante's epic involves a journey of the soul toward God. Virgil, a symbol of human reason, safely guides him through the long, dark descent of hell; and now, at dawn on Easter morning, they finally emerge into the light of purgatory. While hell provided both Dante and the reader a glimpse into the self-destructive nature of sin, purgatory now offers a glimpse into the inner life of the redeemed sinner.

It is the story, really, of a soul who is returning to God and whose desire is compelled by God's love. Dante's literary aspiration was to create a grand epic poem in the tradition of the great classical epics. His work is a mimesis of Virgil's master epic, *Aeneid*. It is important to note that literary mimesis is not imitation; it is emulation at its best. Although Dante admired Virgil more than any other literary figure, he deemed him limited in his scope because he was pagan and failed to grasp truth. Therefore Dante aspired to create a work that would transcend all previous epics—those works that merely glorified men and cultures—and instead celebrate God's redemption of mankind.

While *Inferno* borrows much from Virgil and other writers of classical Greece and Rome, Dante still reworks the mythology for his decidedly Christian purpose. *Purgatorio* and *Pardisio,* however, reflect much more clearly Dante's unique literary style, for the classics offer no pattern for these works. Purgatory is a uniquely Catholic/Christian concept, and the classical Elysian Fields, the unsatisfactory heaven image of Greece and Rome, are represented not in Dante's *Paradiso* but in his Limbo of *Inferno*.

These two canticles introduce brand-new literary patterns and consequently take the epic form to unprecedented heights. Dante's work actually attempts to portray the vastness of the whole Christian canvas, something that had never been done before. Dante's only rival as an epic writer remains the seventeenth-century Puritan writer John Milton. Centuries later Milton sought to do from the Protestant Christian view something similar to what the Catholic Dante had so brilliantly accomplished previously. This progression from Homer to Virgil to Dante to Milton, this great series of poetic achievements, transformed not just the literary landscape, but in many ways the religious landscape as well.

The introduction of Beatrice as Dante's guide in *Purgatorio* signals the reader that Dante is literarily moving beyond his classical predecessors. He depends on Virgil to be his guide only to the highest level that human reason and rationality can take him. So, Virgil guides him through the abyss of hell itself. As they reach purgatory, however, they are joined by Beatrice, Dante's personification of divine love. From their first childhood meeting, she had awakened the deepest longing of his soul. It was a moment that C. S. Lewis would have called *sensucht*, or desire, a desire that really pointed beyond itself to a deeper and more profound aspiration and longing. Left to itself, it would be a false Beatrice (or love), but the true Beatrice, the true image, points beyond itself to the archetype of which it is only an indicator, namely, the love of God.

The historical Beatrice died very young, at age twenty-four, and Dante mourned her loss by writing the *Vita Nuova*, which means "new life." Gradually, however, he numbed to that deepest longing of the soul and began to pursue a love affair of sorts with "Lady Philosophy." It is this error that he must correct through his unearthly pilgrimage recounted in *The Divine Comedy*.

As Dante moves away from the *Inferno*, the poem likewise shifts into a more positive and lyric style in which there seems to be a good deal more joy than grief. In terms of sheer artistry, this second canticle, by comparison to the first one, displays a livelier invention and a greater architectural skill as well as a greater freedom of technique. Dante seems surer now that he has reached this part of the poem. As Sayers says in her commentary on the *Purgatorio*, "The *Inferno* may fill one with only an appalled fascination and the *Paradiso* may daunt one at first by its intellectual severity, but if one is drawn to the *Purgatorio* at all, it is by the chords of love which will not cease drawing until they have drawn the whole poem into the same embrace." In this canticle it is evident that Dante has found his literary way, and with it he continues to carry this great work up to the crescendo that resounds in the higher spheres of paradise itself.

As noted, Dante assigns Beatrice a specific role in this canticle as he leverages that image that was so poignant for him in his youth. Through her, he now moves his reader away from the type to the archetype. Beatrice puts it this way: "I am myself. I am not everything. I am but a type of that which is greater than I." Later, when she has completed her assigned role as his guide, she quietly hands him over to St. Bernard and returns to her own joy in everlasting contemplation. Dante demonstrates through her an idealistic love that can be fraught with various dangers. There is a danger of falling in love with a false image and absolutizing that false image in such a way that it would draw one ever inward into narrowing circles of egotism.

But the image, when understood to be a kind of sacramental vehicle, serves to point beyond itself to the reality. That true image, then, permits one to see beyond oneself and glimpse God. When Dante first beheld Beatrice, he experienced a moment of *ecstasis*, or ecstasy. *Ecstasis* really means to stand outside of oneself and, in that moment when one is no longer preoccupied with self, to be totally consumed with the other. This is really the image of true love, which points beyond concern for oneself and seeks the good of the other. Dante's Beatrician vision is a moment of ecstasy that symbolically points the reader toward the ultimate vision, which is called the beatific, or blessed, vision of God, the crescendo of Dante's third book. To paraphrase Lewis, the longings of the heart that seem to have no earthly fulfillment are merely the hints and shadows of the reality found only in God.

Now in order to fully appreciate Dante's depictions of purgatory, one must grasp something about the nature of evil. Augustine, one of the early church theologians, provided one of the most cogent refutations of a prevalent and problematic religious view that regarded evil as some sort of substance. Instead, he asserted, evil is a parasite that feeds on and distorts the good, a view Tolkien very clearly illustrated in *The Lord of the Rings.* Evil, properly understood, has no creative power; it can only deform the good that already exists. Dante incorporates this Augustinian view of the nature of evil, and therefore every one of purgatory's cornices relates to distorted good and to distorted loves.

It is also important for the reader to grasp that the nature of *Purgatorio* is the permanent orientation of the whole personality toward the good that it persistently pursues. The concept of levity figures significantly in this canticle. Just as the *culpa,* or guilt of sin, was represented in *Inferno* by gravity, the purification from *labis,* or the stain of sin, is represented as levity. As the sinner climbs the mount, he is drawn more and more rapidly toward its pinnacle and God. Dante depicts levity as a positive, irresistible force, just as he uses gravity to depict the downward and destructive pull of sin. While hell exists merely for punishment, purgatory exists solely for purification. Furthermore, purgatory is a place of systematic discipline that is neither arbitrary nor random. While Dante's hell was characterized by chaos, sterility, monotony, and terror, his purgatory is characterized by order, life, purposefulness, and hope.

## Structure of *Purgatorio*

Purgatory then depicts a precise and symmetrical arrangement in which the activity in each circle has significance and value. Dante's challenge, though, was to avoid making purgatory merely an inversion of hell. While he maintains the basic decastructure pattern, *Purgatorio* incorporates a somewhat different numerical system. He dedicates seven cornices to the purging of the seven capital sins, which correlate with the seven deadly sins punished in lower hell. These are preceded by two antipurgatory layers located at the bottom of the mountain. There is yet another layer at the mountain's top, the earthly paradise that was lost as a result of the fall. So, when the two levels of antipurgatory are added to the seven purgational cornices, it adds up to nine, which is the square of three—the number of the Trinity. When the earthly paradise is added to the nine lower levels, the sum is ten, the number of perfection and divine omniscience. While Dante's numerology remains consistent throughout *The Divine Comedy*, he clearly redefines its significance in each canticle.

Dante's two levels of antipurgatory seem to find their correlation in hell's vestibule of opportunists and Limbo. Part of antipurgatory deals with those individuals who repented and turned their hearts toward God just at the moment of death. The other part deals with those who delayed repentance until the moment of death; they are divided into three categories: the indolent, the unshriven, and the preoccupied. Just as they delayed repentance and metaphorically made God wait, they now suffer a period of detention.

Just above antipurgatory is Peter's Gate. Here Dante reminds the reader of the traditional church teaching regarding the three steps of penance: contrition, satisfaction, and confession. Before passing through the gate, Dante receives seven Ps on his forehead, representing *peccatus*, which is the Latin word for "sin." Each of these Ps is erased one by one as he moves upward toward heaven and God. An angel corresponding to each particular level erases each mark as he continues along the path to purification through purgation. We see that in purgatory then, the suffering is not penal but purgative. Each cornice has to do with erasing the stain of sin. These seven root sins presented in *Purgatorio* are not simply symptomatic sins, but rather, in Dante's estimation, the very sources of sin itself.

Good, as discussed earlier, is that which evil feeds on, so it is then logical that Dante should present all the capital sins as deriving from some distortion of good. In the first cornice, he deals with pride. This sin so distorts the love of self that it leads to hatred and contempt for one's neighbor. The next cornice expunges envy, the sin that deals with the perversion of love of oneself to the point of wishing to deprive others of their good. In other words, it is resentment of another's good; the feeling that if you can't have it, they shouldn't either.

A third distortion of love is wrath. Righteous anger

stems from a love of justice, but sinful wrath is perverted into revenge, spite, hate, and unforgiveness. As Dante moves toward midpurgatory, he deals with love that is defective. Here he presents the sin of *acedia*, frequently translated into English as *sloth*. This translation, however, does not adequately communicate the symbolic value Dante assigns to this sin. Accurately understood, this midpoint sin translates as a pivotal spiritual failing: the failure to actively pursue that which is recognized as good. In other words, since all good comes from God, it is a failure to desire to love God. He places it at the midpoint of Mount Purgatory, using it to mark the dividing point between the lower three sins derivating from perverted love and the upper three sins derivating from excessive love.

The three cornices above sloth purgate those sins characterized by excessive love. In the first of these, cornice number five, are the avaricious, those who loved money or power. Above it are the gluttons, those who loved pleasure. Finally, at the highest level, are the lustful. Just as in hell, Dante divided the less egregious sins of impulse from the more vile sins of volition, so in purgatory he places the sins he deems most serious in the lower half of the mount. Notice that the passion sins are nearer the top while the egotistical sins are at the bottom because they exclude reciprocity and exchange with others.

With each cornice there is a corresponding penance appropriate to the sin, either a natural consequence, an effect of the particular sin, or a punishment opposite to the virtue. These cantos also contain a meditation, consisting of what is called the wit, or opposing virtue, which is always taken from the life of Mary or other saints. Dante also includes deterrent examples of each sin to characterize it and illustrate its consequences, and a prayer accompanies each level, a specific benediction taken from the Beatitudes. Finally, presiding angels oversee the sinners contained at the various levels. So there is a very complex structure present throughout the canticle, yet it is so subtly interwoven into the narrative that upon first reading of the poem, it is almost unnoticeable. Dante carefully avoids the trap of pedanticism as his literary architecture unfolds.

At the summit of Mount Purgatory is the earthly paradise, the place of innocence. It remains uninhabited as a result of man's sin, yet ultimately this area will be peopled, indicating that God wastes nothing. In Dante's concept of purgatory, even sin is not wasted.

Here at the very top are two rivers from which Dante drinks. The first is called *Lethe*, and again this image is refurbished from classical imagery. There it was the river of forgetfulness that flowed near Elysium. Those entering that region of the underworld drank from it in order to forget the glories of life—so that they could be satisfied with the monotonies of a paradise without achievement or glory. Dante redeems this image, and in his narrative, a drink from Lethe destroys all memory of evil and the guilt that accompanies it. Later, he drinks from a second river, Euno, which means "good knowledge." In a final purification, this river washes away the knowledge of evil acquired at the fall, leaving only knowledge of the good. Dante is now prepared to enter into heaven, which is paradise itself.

## Symbolism of *Purgatorio*

As Dante moves higher and higher through the cornices of purgatory, the weight of his sin grows lighter, and it becomes easier for him to ascend. Remember that this mountain is supposedly about three thousand miles high. According to Dante, this climb is made possible only through divine intervention and enablement. As Dante submits his will, levity works on him more powerfully, speeding his ascent. Dante uses this symbol to provide a picture of the regenerating work of the Holy Spirit within the life of the Christian.

As purgation gradually erases the stain of sin, Dante's desire for God grows. When he finally reaches the peak of the ascent, this is personified in the presentation of the four maidens, symbols of the four cardinal virtues: justice, prudence, fortitude, and temperance. Now Dante can embrace these God-given virtues instead of sin. They are followed by maidens representing the three theological virtues of faith, hope, and love. At this point, Beatrice's archetypal function becomes fully apparent. The three maidens of theological virtue remove her veil, and for the first time in ten years, Dante sees the glory of her face. Biblically, the rending of the temple veil symbolizes man's accessibility to God through the atoning work of Christ. Clearly, Dante's Beatrice has not only served as a symbol of divine love to lead Dante to this point, but she is a messianic symbol, a Christ type who has led him into relationship with God.

## Introduction to *Paradiso*

It has been said that the joys of heaven are an acquired
taste, and Dante's image of *paradiso* is really a story of how
one acquires that taste. What Dante does so brilliantly is to
engage his reader because we are strangers there in heaven,
and by now Dante at least is known to us. Therefore he becomes a type of ourselves as we vicariously tour his heaven
image. In that very process of wonder, fear, and amazement,
we gradually become more accustomed to this radiant vision.
We observe as Dante's vision of the love of God continues to
grow and strengthen.

Dante displays astonishing courage in his attempt to
create a persuasive image of heaven. It is no small task. To
accomplish the feat, this canticle introduces radically different images and poetic strategies. Indeed, this whole section
is rich with images of light, dance, and music. In the final
spheres, the reader can almost see the sacred dance, the cosmic dance itself, as souls whirl around in concentric spheres,
a depiction of the glories of that love that moves the sun and
the stars. The entire poem builds to an ecstatic climax in this
canticle.

In a letter that Dante wrote later in his life, during his
twenty-year exile from Florence, he dedicated a portion of
his *Paradiso* to one of his patrons. In this epistle, the author
explained how to interpret his work:

> It is meant for the exposition to be both literal
> and allegorical. And so, to make this intel-
> ligible it should be known that writings can
> be understood and ought to be expounded

chiefly in four senses. The first is called literal and that is the sense that does not go beyond the strict limits of the letter. The second sense is called allegorical. This is where we have a truth that is hidden under a beautiful fiction. The third sense is the moral, and that moral sense is what does it teach us for our profit and how should we respond. The fourth sense is what is called anagogic and that speaks of the spiritual exposition.

And so Dante described his work as polysemantic; that is to say, it has many levels of meaning, all of which contribute to the work as a whole. We need to keep this in mind because, as I mentioned earlier, to read Dante's narrative only literally is to miss the larger point of it all—that it is the journey away from unreality and sin into the very source of life and light and love. "To know all things in God" is to know them as they really are. This is Dante's central idea.

## Structure of *Paradiso*

The complexity of the cosmology of Dante's heaven has bewildered many a student of *The Divine Comedy*. It is predicated on a Ptolemaic view of the universe. According to classical belief, the universe was divided into two regions: the earthly or sublunar region and the heavens. The earthly region was vulnerable to change, corruption, and decay, while the heavenly one was immutable and perfect.

According to Aristotelian cosmology, which Ptolemy's model contradicted just slightly, Earth was the fixed center of the sublunar universe, around which the fixed heavenly bodies rotated in circular orbits: the moon, Mercury, Venus, the sun, Mars, Jupiter, and Saturn. Beyond these were the fixed stars, and beyond those, the Prime Mover, who directed the movements of the universe from the outside yet remained unmoved himself. The motions of the planetary bodies were regarded as perfectly spherical and constant, never increasing or decreasing in speed. Within this ordered view of the cosmos, everything had an assigned place and function. Ptolemy's theory differed from Aristotle's in that he argued that the universe's center was not exactly Earth, but he retained the view that planetary motion was circular. Dante used that circularity of motion throughout his epic structure, but nowhere is it more significant than in this third canticle.

Dante divided his heaven into two regions: the visible heavens and the invisible heavens. The outer seven rings compose the visible area and include the moon, Mercury, Venus, Mars, the sun, Jupiter, and Saturn. Dante scholar Rachel Jacoff noted that the first three spheres are situated in the shadow of Earth, a reminder of the imperfections of their resident souls. Beyond Earth's shadow, Dante endowed his souls with a luminosity that reflects their joy. The *primum mobile* is situated between the visible and invisible realms; it is here that Dante's angels/movers exist and work. Beyond this division between the material and immaterial heavens is the transition out of time and into eternity and the presence of God himself.

## Symbolism in *Paradiso*

Critics have typically interpreted Dante's first three spheres of heaven to symbolize particular defects in humanity: inconstancy, pride, and lust. These then correspond to the three theological virtues introduced at the conclusion of *Purgatorio* and later reincorporated into *Paradiso*: faith, hope, and charity. In keeping with his Ptolemaic cosmology, Dante depicts relationship to God through physical location. Just as Satan is located at the farthest reach of the material universe, indicating his spiritual estrangement from God, so the rings or spheres of heaven indicate the soul's proximity to God. Merely by placing a soul in a particular place in his universe, Dante indicates that soul's condition.

The outer spheres of the material universe radiate in the light of God. In the ring of the sun reside the doctors of the church, as well various theologians, and leaders who guided God's church. Mars is the residence of holy warriors, in keeping with the role of Mars as a god of war in classical mythology. Jupiter contains the just rulers, also a fitting reminder of Jupiter's dominion over the upper world in mythology. Saturn is home to the contemplatives, those who dwell in the bliss of spiritual love itself.

From this point, Dante moves the reader toward the starry heavens and ultimately toward what is called the *primum mobile*, or the crystalline heaven, the place from which all movement is directed and beyond which time and space become meaningless concepts.

There he sees the vision of time, a river of light, turning forever into a circle of eternity. He conveys this image as the famous multifoliate rose, the pattern by which he is able to see all things from a kind of a present-tense perspective. Here he departs from the classical imagery in exchange for the biblical, creating a Dantean version of Ezekiel's vision of a wheel within a wheel. Instead of seeing things within the framework of time, in a sequential movement, he provides a vision that synchronizes all time into eternity. He sees that God is not only the center of the universe, but also the center of the soul. He depicts this concept with the dual wheel image. While God exists at the center of the redeemed soul, he also exists as the center of his universe, and man progresses in an eternal, circular rotation around God. In other words, God becomes both the circumference and the center of all that exists in him. Polarity disappears, and the soul exists only within that perpetual union and cosmological relationship. With this image, Dante synthesizes his entire Ptolemaic view.

## Synopsis of *Paradiso*

I want to make a few comments about the organization of Dante's *Paradise*. As previously mentioned, the lower heavens correspond to the four cardinal virtues of fortitude, justice, temperance, and prudence and the three theological virtues of faith, hope, and charity. Dante is even given a quiz on these concepts. Peter, James, and John test and teach him. In fact, each level presents various discourses; these are philosophical and theological discussions on human freedom, the nature of time, the nature of God, and so forth. Scholars have noted that in this aspect of the work, *Paradiso* is the most medieval of the three canticles. Dante does not really describe heaven so much as move the reader into a world of ideas.

Each soul encountered represents various concepts as well. For instance, the first group represents those who were inconstant in their vows but who are now perfected. The second level corresponds to the ambitious. Dante uses the emperor Justinian as an example. He also provides a discourse on justice. The third heaven corresponds to Venus and deals with love. The fourth heaven, that of the sun, is depicted as luminous, and thus theologians are found here.

By the way, from the second heaven on, and moving all the way up through the ninth sphere, there are no actual images of people. They are depicted as insubstantial, almost like points of light. They are visible because of their movements, which cause them to shine in different degrees of brightness.

The fifth heaven, Mars, corresponds to holy warriors and deals with the virtue of fortitude. Charlemagne and William of Orange are offered as examples here. The sixth heaven, Jupiter, corresponds to rulership or leadership. Finally, the seventh heaven, Saturn, presents human action in the context of the contemplative life. Here Dante places Benedict and others.

From this lower grouping of heavenly spheres, Dante ascends the celestial ladder into the eighth heaven, which is the heaven of the fixed stars and the residence of the friends of Christ: the Virgin Mary, St. Peter, St. James, St. John, and even Adam himself. Above that, in the ninth heaven, Dante places the first mover, the *primum mobile*.

These spheres move from angels to archangels, to

principalities, to powers, to virtues, to dominions, to thrones, and on to cherubim and seraphim. For Dante's tenth level, there is no corresponding angel, for here is the empyrean, the abode of God. By this point Beatrice has disappeared, and Dante is now escorted by St. Bernard.

As he sees and experiences each level, Dante's capacity for understanding increases. I think *Paradiso* is likely where C. S. Lewis received the inspiration for the similar image he creates at the end of *The Voyage of the Dawn Treader*. As the characters go toward the sunrise and the east, the light grows brighter and brighter, and the water on which they are sailing looks like liquid light. After a while they sample this water and their eyes become accustomed to the light. The reason I suspect that Lewis borrowed this from Dante is because it is the image of the redeemed becoming fit to abide in the presence of the Holy.

It has been said that Dante's *Inferno* presented a sensory perception of sin, *Purgatorio* an emotional response to sin, and *Paradiso* a visionary glimpse of God. In fact, his poetry is a sort of visual music. He depicts his famous image of three triune, yet distinct, spheres that occupy a single, multidimensional space: Father, Son, and Holy Spirit. He seeks to depict his master image: the image of the convergence of polarity in the soul's union with its Creator. This is the supreme vision, and though he sees it, he cannot fully understand it. High fantasy reaches its limit in the crescendo of *Paradiso*. At that moment, he feels as though his whole being has been reoriented and turned toward God, who is the true center. So, we have this beautiful picture of the movement of the soul toward God, for whom it was created.

It is important to understand that man's union with the heavenly light is not *absorption into* but rather a *reunion with* God. Dante's vision keeps intact the I-thou relationship, the subject and the object, just as there is the I-thou within the Divine Trinity. This is no transcendental collective soul, where identity and personhood are diminished or lost. It is quite the contrary. Dante's image depicts that in the presence of God, the soul will, for the first time, be most fully itself—what it was created to be. The earthly, temporal images give way to and are superseded by reality. Dante's first two canticles relied on representational images, but in God is all reality itself. Representation no longer has a place. This is why Beatrice must recede; her representational role is fulfilled. Imagery is fulfilled.

As we see then, Dante's pilgrimage climaxes in God. Man, while in time, had existed at the midpoint in the universal hierarchy, or ladder of creation. Again, Dante incorporates medieval concepts. The medieval man was aware of a cosmic hierarchy. Man, the midpoint of that hierarchy, possessed a rational soul. Below him were the beasts, the animals, endowed with life—form and instinct—but not rational souls. Below the animal level was the vegetative level, devoid of both soul and instinct, possessing only life and matter and form. Below this existed inorganic matter devoid of life and possessing only form. Finally, at the lowest part of the chain, was prime matter itself, having no form but merely undifferentiated being. Everything below that point, then, becomes a negation of existence, as is the case with hell itself. Again it seems that C. S. Lewis borrowed from this medieval concept in his depiction of the soul in hell in *The*

*Great Divorce*. He asserted that the damned are mere shadows or shades of reality and that hell is as close to nothingness as something can become and yet still exist.

And so, according to this hierarchical view of the created universe, man is the broken rung in the ladder, the only part of creation that rebels against God's purpose. Dante depicted the incarnation as God stepping into time to redeem rebellious man and restore order to his creation. That broken rung is redeemed by the accomplished work of the living Christ, for it is through Christ that God provides the means by which man is brought into the "you in Me, and I in you" relationship (see John 14:20). It is that coinherence alluded to by Charles Williams.

Only in the Christian vision of the Divine Trinity is there a basis for grasping how one can have equality and authority at the same time. Typically, man errs to extremes, elevating authority, to the diminishment of equality, which is totalitarianism; or emphasizing equality at the expense of authority, which becomes egalitarianism. The idea set forth in the Scriptures is the Trinitarian relationship of hierarchy without inferiority.

## Conclusion

Throughout his epic, Dante stresses the dynamic nature of redemption as he moves, really, from a philosophy of *being* to a philosophy of *becoming*. He shows that we can attempt to love the good for the sake of the self, but then it will become an impediment to the soul's joy. Infinitely better, we can learn the secret that Solomon expressed in Ecclesiastes: that nothing can be enjoyed apart from relationship with God. In light of this truth, then, God's good gifts serve as vehicles by which we learn of him and his love for us. God himself must be the chief joy of man.

Before we close our discussion, let me draw your attention to just a few final quotes from this wonderful work. In describing the joys of heaven in the fourth canto of *Paradiso*, Dante says, "Each in the first circle glittereth and all share one sweet life, diversified." Here he makes a very important point. While it appears from this vision that the redeemed souls are differentiated, he depicts them as also sharing one undifferentiated life. This seems to be Dante's attempt to illustrate the mystery of eternal unity without loss of identity.

For the remainder of these quotes, I will refer to the Allen Mandelbaum translation, which I found to be very helpful. In the first canto of *Paradiso,* in describing empyrean heaven, Dante writes, "The glory of the One who moves all things permeates the universe and glows in one part more and another less. I was in the heaven that receives more of His light. And I saw things that he who from that height descends, forgets or cannot speak; for bearing its desired end, our intellect sinks into an abyss so deep that memory fails to follow it." Here he admits his inadequacy to capture the beauty of the beatific vision, despite his poetic skill.

Have you ever experienced something, such as a dream, that was profound in its impact? However, as the experience grows more distant, its significance and impact begin to elude you? That is the type of experience Dante laments here. C. S. Lewis also addressed this sort of experience, asserting that sometimes we have "good dreams." He felt that much of mythology fit into that category—corrupted memories, so to speak, of what was lost at the fall.

In any case, our capacity is bound now. While bound in time, we see through a glass darkly, but someday, as Scripture promises, we will see face to face and "know fully just as I also have been fully known" (1 Corinthians 13:12).

In the second canto, Dante writes, "If I was body (and on earth we cannot see how things material can share one space—the case when body enters body), then should our longing be still more inflamed to see that Essence in which we discern how God and human nature were made one. What we hold here by faith shall there be seen, not demonstrated but directly known." Again Dante anticipates that great day when faith will become fact, when images will give way to reality. He then goes on to note,

> We do not thirst for greater blessedness, should we desire a higher sphere than ours then our desires would be discordant with the will of Him who has assigned us here. But you will see no such discord in these spheres. To live and love is here a necessity. The essence of this blessed life consists in keeping to the boundaries of God's will for which our wills become one single will so that we are raised from step to step throughout this Kingdom. All this Kingdom wills that which will please the King whose will is to rule and in whose will there is our peace.

Clearly, he longs for that time when the human will can

rest in the perfect will of God, without sinful impediments. Then, in perhaps one of the better-known lines from *Paradiso*, Dante adds, "And in whose will there is our peace." What a beautiful definition of peace—resting in God's presence and will!

Related to this concept, Dante had elsewhere noted, "Only Man's sin annuls Man's liberty. It makes him unlike the highest good so that in him the brightness of its light is dimmed and Man cannot regain his dignity unless where sin left emptiness Man fills that void with just amends for evil pleasure." "For no obedience, no humility," he offered later, "could have been so deep that it could match the heights he meant to reach through disobedience." Here he identifies the very problem that prohibits true peace; in the futility of attempting to exercise liberty, man annuls it. Glorification will be the restoration of the will to its proper state of submission to God. The void created by sin will be filled with God himself.

Dante emphasizes that man lacks the power to secure his own peace. That is why, he says, "the Godly goodness of the world was happy to proceed through both its ways to raise you up again. For God showed greater generosity in giving His own self that Man might be able to rise than if He simply pardoned; for every other means fell short of justice except the way by which the Son of God humbled Himself when He became incarnate." That is good theology.

Dante goes so far as to envision what the reunion of the soul with God will be: "Then like a clock that calls us at the hour, the bride of God, awakening, sings matins to her bridegroom, encouraging His love and each clock part both drives and draws, chiming the sounds of notes so sweet that those with spirit well disposed feel their love grow. So did I see the wheel that moved in glory, go round and render voice to voice to such sweetness and such accord that they cannot be known except where joy is everlasting." He crafts a beautiful metaphor here.

I will conclude with Dante's discussion of the grace of God: "O grace abounding, through which I presumed to set my eyes on the Eternal Light, so long that I spent all my sight on it. In this profundity I saw—ingathered and bound in love into one single volume—what, in the universe, seems separate, scattered: substances, accidents and dispositions as if conjoined—in such a way that what I tell is only rudimentary. I think I saw the universal shape which that knot takes."

He then ends the work by describing the circles that I mentioned earlier:

> In the deep and bright essence of that exalted light, three circles appeared to me; they had three different colors, but all of them were of the same dimension; one circle seemed reflected by the second, as rainbow is by rainbow, and the third seemed fire breathed equally by those two circles. How incomplete is speech, how weak, when set against my thought! And this, to what I saw is such—to call it little is too much. Eternal Light, You only dwell within Yourself, and only You know You; Self-knowing, Self-known, You love and smile upon Yourself.

Again he laments his inability to convey his vision of the glory of God. It is similar to a moment related in the Book of Job, after God has spoken to Job and revealed aspects of his power and glory. In response to what he hears and understands, Job humbly states, "Behold, I am insignificant; what can I reply to You? I lay my hand on my mouth" (Job 40:4). Dante concludes by saying, "Here force failed my high fantasy; but my desire and will were moved already—like a wheel revolving uniformly—by the Love that moves the sun and other stars."

Triune God, I marvel at the beauty and uniqueness of your pursuit of us in Christ to deliver us from the bondage and consequences of sin. You have given me hope in this transient world as an inheritor of love, life, and light in your eternal kingdom. May I pursue you above all earthly goods and find my deep pleasure in your presence. In Jesus' name. Amen.

# NOTES

# The Knowledge of the Holy

## Introduction

A. W. Tozer, often described as a twentieth century prophet, was a man whose work and preaching were anointed by God because he knew God by way of acquaintance and not by hearsay. His two great classics, in my opinion, are *The Pursuit of God* and *The Knowledge of the Holy*. Tozer was born in 1897 and died in the same year as C. S. Lewis, 1963. Both men were prominent Christian writers and were aware of each other's work. Tozer became a very well-respected pastor and author by the end of his life. Billy Graham often sought his counsel, as did Mark Hatfield, and he exchanged regular correspondence with Thomas Merton as well.

He was an extraordinary man who depended on a diversity of resources. Although he was affiliated with the Christian and Missionary Alliance, a very conservative denomination, nevertheless he exposed himself to a wide range of unusual books—books by people he called "friends of God." Some of these were books that dated back to the ancient world as well as the medieval period; others were by Puritan and Reformation authors, as well as authors of his own time. He looked for people who really understood God in a deep and intimate way. Such writers resonated with him and influenced him profoundly. Despite the fact that he had no formal higher-level education, his reading was extensive. Ironically, he spent only one day in high school and then determined he would be better served by self-education—something he took seriously. He studied philosophy and the classics, and it has been said that he would sometimes read Shakespeare on his knees, praying for God to help him understand.

With time and effort, he became an accomplished wordsmith, and perhaps because of his unconventional pursuit of education, he thought and wrote quite differently from the typical mold of seminary graduates. He was an independent thinker who eagerly explored truth in many forms and venues.

Tozer's study always began and ended with prayer; he regarded prayer as the fundamental component for the preparation of his sermons. He once quipped, "I pray like a Calvinist; but I preach like an Arminian." He became known as a man who was always ready to minister to those who hungered for God, yet he had no time for people who really weren't serious about knowing and following God. As might be expected from these descriptions of him, he largely walked alone in life, interacting with only a very tiny circle of friends. He was an unconventional minister, for he also tended to avoid interaction with people, some might even say to a fault. He had a habit of coming into church at the singing of the first stanza of the opening hymn and leaving during the last stanza of the closing hymn.

It was also understood that he would never visit hospitalized members of his congregation unless the person was on the verge of death. Once when he was returning from a trip, he drove by the hospital and decided to stop and visit someone. When he arrived in the man's room, the poor fellow became petrified with fear and exclaimed, "Has the doctor not told me something here? It must be worse than I thought. If Tozer's here, it's the kiss of death." Clearly, he had some eccentricities as a pastor.

His remarkable life is best illustrated, however, by his ordination covenant, one that he took very seriously. This was a covenant he wrote himself; later he formalized and published it in one of the first issues of *Alliance Life*, a church magazine that he edited for many years. In that covenant he wrote,

> Forbid that I should become a religious scribe and thus lose my prophetic calling. Save me from the curse that lies dark across the face of the modern clergy; the curse of compromise; of imitation; and of professionalism. Save me from the error of judging a church by its size, its popularity, or the amount of its yearly offerings. Help me to remember that I am a prophet; not a promoter; not a religious manager, but a prophet. Let me never become a slave to crowds. Heal my soul of carnal ambitions and deliver me from the itch of publicity. Save me from bondage to things.

At the conclusion of the covenant he vowed, "And now O Lord of heaven and earth, I consecrate my remaining days to You. Let them be many or few, as Thou will. Let me stand before the great or minister to the poor and lowly. That is Your choice and not mine; and I would not influence it if I could. I am Thy servant to do Thy will; and that will is sweeter to me than position, or riches, or fame. I choose it above all things on earth or in heaven."

He meant what he said, and God greatly blessed his ministry. It was marked by qualities that I find to be extremely rare in modern culture. He was not impressed by the things that impress most believers. He was not a man of his times at all; rather, he was a man who transcended his time and who drank deeply from the well of great writers and thinkers and prophets—people who were close to God. He refused to play any kind of spiritual games, which helped him remain a shrewd and careful judge of his own generation. It would be very interesting, if Tozer were in our midst today, to see what he would think of the contemporary church. I fear he would find it extremely shallow and Laodicean in nature.

I want to provide a sort of guided tour of Tozer's *The Knowledge of the Holy*, yet let the book speak for itself. This book is really a meditative and devotional examination of the attributes of God. Though it is good theology, it is not only that; Tozer is very precise in his thinking, but his book offers a description of his own personal understanding of God. It gives us access into a perspective that so inflamed and energized this man's life.

Tozer offers a balanced presentation of the various attributes of God in this book, but I would point out here at the beginning that we live in a time when our culture is becoming increasingly selective as to which attributes of God merit emphasis. I find more and more books describing God's goodness, love, compassion, and mercy, but fewer and fewer that acknowledge his divine omniscience, omnipotence, transcendence, justice, holiness, or sovereignty. Many seek to diminish God and reduce him to their comfort level. The kind of God many people imagine is only a distorted image, insofar as they selectively accept some attributes—the desirable attributes—and eliminate those that conflict with their notion of God. They want him to be immanent but not transcendent.

Too many people, Christians included, have bought into a culture that is dumbing down theology and diminishing the biblical vision of God as holy and awesome, yet intimate and close. He is both immanent and transcendent; he is to be loved, but also to be feared, and these categories are mutually reinforcing. C. S. Lewis also noticed this tendency to confuse and ignore the aspects of God's character that make us uncomfortable, along with our inclination to believe that some of his qualities conflict with others. In his children's book *The Lion, the Witch and the Wardrobe,* Lucy becomes alarmed when she learns that the king of the land of Narnia she is visiting is a lion. Lucy then questions fearfully, "Then he isn't safe?" To which the more knowledgeable Mr. Beaver responds, "Safe? . . . 'Course he isn't safe. But he's good. He's the King, I tell you" (chap. 7). Tozer and Lewis both well understood what we all need to grasp: God is who he is, and we need to come to know him in truth. Our misperceptions will not alter God; they will harm only us.

Now, in my opinion, Tozer's opening preface to *The Knowledge of the Holy* is worth the price of the book. He begins this way: "True religion confronts earth with heaven and brings eternity to bear upon time." He goes on to assert that there has been "the loss of the concept of majesty from the popular religious mind. The Church has surrendered her once lofty concept of God and has substituted for it one so low, so ignoble, as to be utterly unworthy of thinking, worshiping men. This she has done not deliberately, but little by little and without her knowledge; and her very unawareness only makes her situation all the more tragic." Just what is he saying here? He is saying that in a very gradual way, we have bought into the mindset of our time and imposed it on Scripture. In some cases, our culture has now so distorted our vision of God and the truth of his Word that it has attempted to reduce God and attempted to tame him.

"With our loss of the sense of majesty," Tozer writes, "has come the further loss of religious awe, and consciousness of the divine Presence. We have lost our spirit of worship and our ability to draw inwardly to meet God in adoring silence." If this were true when he wrote it a number of decades ago, how much more appropriate is it today to say that we have lost the sense of true awe, wonder, and majesty?

Bear in mind, and Tozer will support this, it is good to be "both-and" in our thinking about the attributes of God. God's attributes as presented in Scripture do not conflict or compete with one another. In a paradoxical sense, he is near and far; holy and majestic and terrifying; just and demanding yet also intimate—closer than we can imagine—"you in Me, and I in you" (John 14:20). It is not a question of one versus the other; it is the case of taking the full counsel of Scripture and merging it together into a coherent whole.

## Thinking Rightly about God

In the book's first chapter, "Why We Must Think Rightly about God," Tozer opens with a prayer. The rich prayers that begin each chapter to the book are so wonderful that they inspired me to create a DVD called *The Prayers of A. W. Tozer*. I combined the prayers that begin each of these chapters with the prayers that conclude each chapter in *The Pursuit of God*. I then meshed them together into a single DVD and added contemplative music and exquisite photographic images from God's creation. Tozer's prayers provide a rich devotional exercise. (This contemplative DVD is available on my KenBoa.org website.)

Here is one of those prayers: "They that know Thee not may call upon Thee as other than Thou art, and so worship not Thee but a creature of their own fancy; therefore enlighten our minds that we may know Thee as Thou art, so that we may perfectly love Thee and worthily praise Thee." Here he notes the danger of worshiping a God of our "own fancy," our own making. The first sentence of the chapter's text is also critical to understanding not only the mind of Tozer but also the thesis of the entire book. He declares, "What comes into our minds when we think about God is the most important thing about us." That is a very profound statement. His desire in writing this book was to expand the Christian's vision of who God really is, for as our understanding expands, our capacity to worship him properly also expands.

It is my conviction that part of our calling, as we allow God to define us, and as we strive to comprehend the mysteries of God, is to commit all that we know about ourselves to all that we know about God. That process should not be static; it should be dynamic. The ideal here is that we would continue to know God better and, as we get to know him better, see ourselves more and more as he sees us.

That process, then, should endure throughout this whole journey of life. The problem is that many times we stop expanding our vision of God. In fact, when we do that, we diminish him and turn away from him. Tozer writes, "We tend by a secret law of the soul to move toward our mental image of God." I believe that is right. Whether it is away from or closer to the true God of Scripture will depend on how we feed and renew our minds, what we expose ourselves to, the people with whom we associate, and the books we read. Without doubt, the mightiest thought the mind can entertain is the thought of God, and the weightiest word in any language is the name of God.

Therefore, right at the beginning of this book, Tozer declares that we must start by thinking rightly about God. When we do that, we are able to begin to move in a direction that will be honoring and pleasing to him. Tozer asserts, "I believe that there is scarcely an error in doctrine or a failure in applying Christian ethics that cannot be traced finally to imperfect and ignoble thoughts about God." That is quite a statement to make. He is saying that our vision and our knowledge of the holy must necessarily shape our behavior, our apprehension, our desire, our aspirations, our intentions, and, indeed, all aspects of life.

Thus, Tozer hates—he loathes—the sin of idolatry. He describes it this way: "The idolatrous heart assumes God is other than He is—in itself a monstrous sin—and substitutes for the true God one made after its own likeness." The approach that we see in religious apprehension is somehow to reduce the idea of God as revealed in the natural world down to proportions that are not terrifying, but manageable as well as controllable. We even do the same thing to the Scriptures—we reduce them to manageable proportions, a level we falsely believe we can control and influence.

It is almost as if prayer suddenly becomes some magical formula, and we suppose that we can get God to do what we want if only we say the right words in the right way. Such faulty thinking becomes a volatile compound, and all kinds of prosperity gospel thinking emerge: "name it and claim it," "believe it and receive it," "blab it and grab it," and "confess and possess."

Indeed, I often describe these prayers as a kind of strategy session that we negotiate with God, whereby we tell God what we believe our best interests to be and then give him generous suggestions as to when and how he can pull off our demands. Of course this would be anathema to Tozer, who would argue that true prayer ought to be a matter of communing in God's presence and inviting the Spirit of God to reveal his desires and words. He would say that we should, like young Samuel, be ready to respond, "Speak, LORD, for Your servant is listening." Thus, he says, "the essence of idolatry is the entertainment of thoughts about God that are unworthy of Him."

## God Incomprehensible

In the second chapter, Tozer moves into the topic of "God Incomprehensible." I am pleased that he wrote these early chapters prior to launching into the actual attributes of God, for he prepares us to understand as he shows us that God is incomprehensible. In the third chapter, he defines just exactly what a divine attribute is, and it is only when we reach the fourth chapter that we actually move into the exploration of the nature of the Holy Trinity. Tozer does not actually introduce the attributes themselves until chapter five, where he discusses the self-existence of God.

Getting back to chapter two, his chapter on the in-comprehensibility of God, Tozer writes, "God is not like anything; that is, He is not exactly like anything or anybody." This is very important for us to grasp; he is knowable, yet we cannot fully know him. We can love him and have a relation-ship with him, yet he transcends our comprehension. He is entirely *unknowable* in his essence and in his nature. The only way we can know him at all is through that which he chooses to reveal to us. Tozer describes, for example, how Ezekiel saw heaven opened and beheld visions of God and found himself looking at that which he had no language to describe. In relating Ezekiel's encounter, Tozer writes, "The nearer he approaches to the burning throne the less sure his words become." I would invite you to read Ezekiel chapter one as an illustration of this meeting that he has with the power and the majesty of the living God. Tozer continues, "So, in order to convey the idea of what he sees, the prophet must employ such words as 'likeness,' 'appearance,' 'as it were,' and 'the likeness of the appearance.' Even the throne becomes 'the appearance of a throne' and He that sits upon it, though like a man, is so unlike that He can be described only as the 'like-ness of the appearance of a man.'"

You see how Ezekiel is at the end of his wit and descriptive power? No words will suffice to encompass and comprehend this vision. Indeed, we see the same kind of language being used in the prologue to the Gospel of John and in his description of the Revelation of Jesus Christ. John is at the limit of his comprehension, and the words then become highly symbolic, and we cannot fully grasp what is happening in this vision. Tozer writes, "Left to ourselves we tend immediately to reduce God to manageable terms. We want to get Him where we can use Him, or at least know where He is when we need Him. We want a God we can in some measure control." With this statement, Tozer is spot on. Once again, I think that his words are perhaps more true in our age—the twenty-first century—than they were in his own century, and they ring true with regard to the state of the church.

Tozer also affirms, "In Christ and by Christ, God effects complete self-disclosure, although He shows Himself not to reason but to faith and love. Faith is an organ of knowledge, and love an organ of experience." We cannot approach God merely through cognition. This is not to diminish the need for clear thinking, and Tozer surely believed in propositional thought and valued reason. But Tozer was also aware of the limits and the boundaries of human cognition. He followed the example of Paul, who, in writing to the Ephesians, prayed that they would come to know the love of God that surpasses all knowledge; that they would have a spirit of wisdom and of revelation in the knowledge of him; that the eyes of their hearts would be enlightened; and that they could know that which they could otherwise not know. The organ for this is really love and faith—trusting in him.

Tozer expands on this and tells us, "The yearning to know what cannot be known, to comprehend the Incomprehensible, to touch and taste the Unapproachable, arises from the image of God in the nature of man. Deep calleth unto deep, and though polluted and landlocked by the mighty disaster theologians call the fall, the soul senses its origin and longs to return to its Source." I fear that our own educational system would seek to diminish that sense of our deepest longings and inspire us to suppose that our deepest felicity is to be found in the pleasures of this passing world.

Continuing, Tozer writes, "What is God like? If by that question we mean 'what is God like in *Himself*,' there is no answer. If we mean 'what has God disclosed *about Himself* that the reverent reason can comprehend,' there is, I believe, an answer both full and satisfying. For while the name of God is secret and His essential nature incomprehensible, He in condescending love has by revelation declared certain things to be true of Himself. These we call His attributes."

It begins to become evident from that statement just exactly how Tozer is approaching his subject. He is preparing the reader for this material. He recommends that instead of just launching into our private prayers, the prudent course would be to pause and reflect on the One we are addressing before we go into his presence and to recognize what a great privilege it is to draw near to the throne of God.

## Divine Attributes

In chapter three, Tozer begins his discussion of attributes by defining the term. He explains with simplicity that a divine attribute is something true about God: "For the purpose of this book *an attribute of God is whatever God has in any way revealed as being true of Himself*" (italics mine). He then goes on to say, "If an attribute is something true of God, it is also something that we can conceive as being true of Him. God, being infinite, must possess attributes about which we can know nothing."

I believe that is an important insight as well; there are so many things that we cannot even begin to know about God. Even if he were to reveal more, we wouldn't have the ability to comprehend. Therefore, he offers us glimpses into this mystery that, someday perhaps, in the bliss and felicitude of heaven, we will be privileged to enter into as we ever so slowly apprehend and acknowledge the glory of the Holy One. I believe all eternity will not be enough for us to plumb the depths of that mystery. Thus, there will always be mysteries and new insights; and each new aspect of himself that he reveals will illuminate something that we had not thought of before. It would be very foolish to suppose that heaven will be boring!

Speaking on this issue of mystery, Tozer says, "To our questions God has provided answers; not all the answers, certainly, but enough to satisfy our intellects and ravish our hearts. These answers He has provided in nature, in the Scriptures, and in the person of His Son." He is telling us that God has given us three real sources of knowledge: the natural world, which is general revelation; Scripture, which is special revelation; and the incarnational revelation, the highest form of revelation in which he became one of us. That is why Jesus could say in effect, "To love me is to love my Father. To see me is to see my Father. To trust in me is to trust in my Father." Every attribute we see in Christ Jesus is a revelation of his Father as well.

Continuing on this discussion of man's limited perception, Tozer writes, "However brightly the light may shine; it can be seen by only those who are spiritually prepared to receive it." This is a very important theme in Tozer's writing. As much as we might desire to know the mysteries of God, they will be closed, even to the ardent theologian, unless one approaches him with humility, faith, love, and under the guidance of the Holy Spirit.

Tozer continues to explain, saying, "Between His attributes no contradiction can exist. He need not suspend one to exercise another, for in Him all His attributes are one. All of God does all that God does; He does not divide Himself to perform work, but works in the total unity of His being." Here he emphasizes "the divine attributes of what we know to be true of God. He does not possess them as qualities; they are how God is as He reveals Himself to His creatures. Love, for instance, is not something that God has and which may grow or diminish or cease to be. His love is the way God is, and when He loves He is simply being Himself. And so with the other attributes."

Tozer points out that God is the ultimate foundation for those qualities that we call the true virtues. He is the ultimate for the true, the beautiful, and the good; they are not something external to him. God is accountable to no one but himself. His unchanging perfection is the absolute foundation of all the concepts we call love and beauty and truth and goodness and mercy and grace and justice and holiness and sovereignty.

## The Holy Trinity

In the fourth chapter Tozer moves on to a discussion of the Holy Trinity, and he observes that "some persons who reject all they cannot explain have denied that God is a Trinity." The error here, of course, is that people try to limit God according to the capability of their own cognition, and that is a dangerous thing to do. Yet Tozer goes on to assert that "every man throughout his entire life constantly accepts without understanding." In other words, there are many aspects of life that we cannot grasp or fully explain, and ironically, while we accept some limitations, when it comes to God we often use our elevated view of our own reasoning ability as an excuse to reduce God to manageable size. The idea of the Trinity, as with so many apparently inexplicable attributes, makes sense if we worship a God who is beyond our grasp and who reveals truths beyond our limited ability to understand. To believe that we should be able to fully comprehend God would be to anthropomorphize him as the classical world did with its false gods. They created gods in their own image—gods whom they could understand and in some cases surpass. Such is not the case with the one true God.

Tozer continues his argument, saying, "Secularism, materialism, and the intrusive presence of things have put out the light in our souls and turned us into a generation of zombies. We cover our deep ignorance with words, but we are ashamed to wonder, we are afraid to whisper 'mystery.'" He then says, "What God declares the bleeding heart confesses without the need for further proof. Indeed, to seek proof is to admit doubt, and to obtain proof is to render faith superfluous." In other words, man has no right to sit in judgment of what is written in Scripture, but rather we must respond to it with faith and humility. He goes on to explain, "The persons of the Godhead, being one, have one will. They work always together, and never one smallest act is done by one without the instant acquiescence of the other two." He goes on to describe how this is also true in creation, in the incarnation, in Christ's baptism, in atonement, in the resurrection, and in the indwelling of his children.

As he describes it, then, the Trinity is a truth that had to be revealed—no one could have imagined such a concept—and I want to stress that no one ever did. It is utterly unique—the idea of God being three in one, perfect in union, three persons who are coequal and coeternal, each fully God, but not each other. It is a deep mystery, but it is the only ontological basis we have for relationships, for community, for society, and for love.

## God's Self-Existence

Next Tozer moves into a discussion of the self-existence of God. He begins with the child's question of where did God come from as "unwittingly acknowledging his creaturehood. The little philosopher is thinking in true creature-idiom and, allowing for his lack of basic information, he is reasoning correctly. The idea here is that we try to divide God into space and time; and to think in ways and categories that we cannot grasp."

He continues, "To think steadily of that to which the idea of origin cannot apply is not easy, if indeed it is possible at all. Just as under certain conditions a tiny point of light can be seen, not by looking directly at it but by focusing the eyes slightly to one side, so it is with the idea of the Uncreated." Then he says, "Only by faith and love are we able to glimpse Him as He passes by our shelter in the cleft of the rock."

He then explains the necessity for humility as we approach God: "To admit that there is One who lies beyond us, who exists outside all our categories, who will not be dismissed with a name, who will not appear before the bar of our reason, nor submit to our curious inquiries: this requires a great deal of humility, more than most of us possess, so we save face by thinking God down to our level, or at least down to where we can manage Him."

Tozer is devoted to this theme, and he develops it carefully. Again he writes, "All of our problems and solutions are theological." He then alludes to the self-existence of God, saying, "Man for all his genius is but an echo of the original Voice, a reflection of the uncreated Light." He goes on to use John chapter one, Hebrews chapter one, and Colossians chapter one to illustrate how everything that exists comes from God—from him, through him, and for him.

## God's Self-Sufficiency

I want to turn now to his prayer at the beginning of chapter six, titled "The Self-Sufficiency of God." He writes, "Teach us, O God, that nothing is necessary to Thee. Were anything necessary to Thee that thing would be the measure of Thine imperfection: and how could we worship one who is imperfect? If nothing is necessary to Thee, then no one is necessary, and if no one, then not we. Thou dost seek us;

though Thou dost not need us. We seek Thee because we need Thee, for in Thee we live and move and have our being." What a wonderful image. "Need," he adds, "is a creature word and cannot be spoken of the Creator. God has a voluntary relation to everything He has made, but He has no necessary relation to anything outside of Himself."

He continues, "Almighty God, just because He is Almighty, needs no support. The picture of a nervous, ingratiating God fawning over men to win their favor is not a pleasant one. Too many missionary appeals are based upon this fancied frustration of Almighty God. An effective speaker can easily excite pity in his hearers, not only for the heathen but for the God who has tried so hard and so long to save them and has failed for want of support." I must admit I have heard lots of sermons that fit that description.

Tozer continues, "I fear that thousands of young persons enter Christian service from no higher motive than to deliver God from the embarrassing situation His love has gotten Him into and His limited abilities seem unable to get Him out of." Frankly, this is too close to the truth. His point, of course, is that God needs no defenders. When we commit ourselves to serving God, it is we who benefit, not him. Tozer then goes on to declare, "Man's only claim to importance is that he was created in the divine image; in himself he is nothing." Our importance is derivative; God's love for us, not our own ability, is what defines us.

## God's Eternality

Moving on to the chapter "The Eternity of God," Tozer says, "Time marks the beginning of created existence, and because God never began to exist it can have no application to Him. 'Began' is a time-word, and can have no personal meaning of the high and lofty One that inhabiteth eternity. God dwells in eternity but time dwells in God. He has already lived all our tomorrows as He has lived all our yesterdays."

## God's Infinitude

The next chapter, "God's Infinitude," begins with the following prayer: "Our heavenly Father, let us see Thy glory, if it must be from the shelter of the cleft rock and beneath the protection of Thy covering hand. Whatever the cost to us in loss of friends or goods or length of days let us know Thee as Thou art, that we may adore Thee as we should through Jesus Christ our Lord." This is the prayer of a passionate man; and, let us be honest, it is difficult to pray that sincerely. When Tozer speaks of God's infinitude, that word implies his limitlessness and the fact that he has no boundaries—that there are no degrees in God. He writes, "In the awful abyss of the divine being may lie attributes of which we know nothing and which can have no meaning for us, just as the attributes of mercy and grace can have no personal meaning for seraphim or cherubim." He is saying that the reason for our dilemma is that we are trying to envision a mode that is altogether foreign to us and wholly unlike anything we have known in our familiar world of matter, energy, space, and time. His love and his nature are boundless and measureless.

In that same chapter, Tozer writes, "The days and years of our lives are few, and swifter than a weaver's shuttle." I have frequently quoted that statement by Tozer, for I am very fond of it. He then continues, "Life is a short and fevered rehearsal for a concert we cannot stay to give. Just when we appear to have attained some proficiency we are forced to lay our instruments down. There is simply not enough time to think, to become, to perform what the constitution of our natures indicates we are capable of." This statement reminds us of the finite existence to which we are confined here on earth. He then contrasts our state with God's, saying, "How completely satisfying to turn from our limitations to a God who has none. Eternal years lie in His heart. For Him time does not pass, it remains; and those who are in Christ share with Him all the riches of limitless time and endless years. God never hurries. There are no deadlines against which He must work. Only to know this is to quiet our spirits and relax our nerves." While we may fear time and its limitations, Tozer offers a poignant reminder that even time is governed by our sovereign Father, whose love is measureless and boundless. The loss of control we sometimes feel subsides when we relinquish ourselves and our cares to our boundlessly capable God.

## God's Immutability

In a chapter on the immutability of God, Tozer continues that exploration of God, asserting that God "never differs from Himself. God cannot change for the better. Neither can God change for the worse. The immutability of God appears in its most perfect beauty when viewed against the mutability of men." Again, time and its ravages are reminders of our finite natures and the fact that we are "in constant flux," but God himself is beyond that world of change and decay.

"Instinctively," Tozer argues, man "seeks the unchanging

and is bereaved at the passing of dear familiar things." In other words, there is a certain longing because of the image of God in us; we long for the immutable; we long for that which does not age, decay, or wear out. We long for something that remains stable. Tozer appeals to that longing by awakening in his readers a longing for that day when we will dwell in the presence of the immutable God in whose image we have been made.

## Divine Omniscience

In his chapter discussing divine omniscience, Tozer begins with a very scriptural prayer: "Lord, Thou knowest all things. Thou knowest my downsitting and mine uprising and art acquainted with all my ways. I can inform Thee of nothing and it is vain to try to hide anything from Thee. In the light of Thy perfect knowledge I would be as artless as a little child. Help me to put away all care, for Thou knowest the way that I take and when Thou hast tried me I shall come forth as gold."

In the course of that chapter, he reminds us that "God knows instantly and effortlessly all matter and all matters, all mind and every mind, all spirit and all spirits, all being and every being, all creaturehood and all creatures, all plurality and all pluralities, all law and every law, all relations, all causes, all thoughts, all mysteries, all enigmas, all feeling, all desires, every unuttered secret, all thrones and dominions, all personalities, all things visible and invisible in heaven and in earth, motion, space, time, life, death, good, evil, heaven, and hell." He says, "No talebearer can inform on us, no enemy can make an accusation stick." This is a very comforting thought. Although the omniscience of God can also be frightening, there is comfort in knowing that all our needs and fears and failings are already known to him.

The One who loves us most is the One who knows us best. Those two go hand in hand; there are no secrets before him. Furthermore, since God knows us best, there is nothing we can hide from him. That is the very truth David meditates on in Psalm 139—that God knows us and also cares for us as no one else can. In that psalm, David implores God, saying, "Search me, O God, and know my heart; try me and know my anxious thoughts; and see if there be any hurtful way in me, and lead me in the everlasting way" (vv. 23–24).

## God's Wisdom

In his chapter concerning the wisdom of God, Tozer writes, "Wisdom, among other things, is the ability to devise perfect ends and to achieve those ends by the most perfect means. It sees the end from the beginning, so there can be no need to guess or conjecture. Wisdom sees everything in focus, each in proper relation to all, and is thus able to work toward predestined goals with flawless precision." Here he extols the wisdom of God and that God gives us a "providential understanding of our circumstances that work for our greatest good and our everlasting well-being." Tozer says that we must "repudiate our own wisdom and take instead the infinite wisdom of God" and that we would do well "to trust Him in the dark," in those areas we do not understand, because of what he has already revealed about himself.

He concludes the chapter by saying, "With the goodness

of God to desire our highest welfare, the wisdom of God to plan it, and the power of God to achieve it, what do we lack? Surely we are the most favored of all creatures." What he acknowledges is so true, yet we rarely act in accordance with that truth. How often do we forget the wisdom and power of God and his sufficiency to care for us?

## God's Omnipotence

Concerning the omnipotence of God, Tozer writes, "He gives but He does not give away. All that He gives remains His own and returns to Him again. Forever He must remain what He has forever been, the Lord God omnipotent." Isn't this an amazing reality? God is never depleted; His power is never diminished. Tozer continues, "Since He has at His command all the power in the universe, the Lord God omnipotent can do anything as easily as anything else. All His acts are done without effort. He expends no energy that must be replenished. His self-sufficiency makes it unnecessary for Him to look outside of Himself for a renewal of strength. All the power required to do all that He wills to do lies in undiminished fullness in His own infinite being." Here Tozer's words reflect an intimate knowledge of the God of whom he writes—not hearsay, not speculation, not the head knowledge of an armchair theologian—but the understanding of a man who speaks out of intimate relationship with a holy God.

## Divine Transcendence

In a brief discussion on divine transcendence, Tozer explains that we must acknowledge God's transcendence in the fullest meaning of that word. He states, "Forever God stands apart, in light unapproachable. He is as high above an archangel as above a caterpillar, for the gulf that separates the archangel from the caterpillar is but finite, while the gulf between God and the archangel is infinite." The fact of God's transcendence is one that we often fail to consider. It is a quality of his character that is powerfully conveyed in Job 42:2–3, where Job humbly states, "I know that You can do all things, and that no purpose of Yours can be thwarted. 'Who is this that hides counsel without knowledge?' Therefore I have declared that which I did not understand, things too wonderful for me, which I did not know." What a powerful contrast exists between the limited nature of finite man and the unlimited nature of an eternal God!

Tozer then observes the inherent danger in forgetting God's transcendent nature: "When the psalmist saw the transgression of the wicked, his heart told him how it could be. 'There is no fear of God before his eyes,' he explained, and in so saying revealed to us the psychology of sin. When men no longer fear God, they transgress His laws without hesitation." Our postmodern culture is moving further and further away from an understanding or acknowledgment of divine transcendence. There is a loss of the sense or conception of God as awesome and dreadful. Yet we see in Scripture that whenever God appeared to people in biblical times, the response was the same; there was "an overwhelming sense of terror and dismay, a wrenching sense of sinfulness and guilt." Tozer refers to Abram, Moses, Isaiah, and Daniel, all of whom humbled themselves before a God they recognized as holy and omnipotent. This healthy fear as seen in Scripture is hardly found today in Christian men and women.

## God's Omnipresence

In Tozer's chapter titled "God's Omnipresence," he quotes Hildebert of Lavardin, a medieval Catholic bishop, who wrote, "God is over all things and under all things; outside all; within but not enclosed; without but not excluded; above but not raised up; below but not depressed; wholly above, presiding; wholly beneath, sustaining; wholly within, filling." Tozer attempts to convey that God's omnipresence is beyond our limited grasp. He tells us the reality is this: "God is, and God is here." It all comes down to that truth, which is "to the convinced Christian a source of deep comfort in sorrow and of steadfast assurance in all the varied experiences of his life." What a comforting thought to remember that God is always with us—that he is, as the psalmist wrote, "our refuge and strength, a very present help in trouble. Therefore we will not fear, though the earth should change and though the mountains slip into the heart of the sea; though its waters roar and foam, though the mountains quake at its swelling pride" (46:1–3). With these words, we are reminded that when we rest in the care of our omnipresent Father, we have nothing to fear. This experience that Scripture relates is not visionary; it is real as we practice his presence—the omnipresence of the living God.

## God's Faithfulness

Concerning God's faithfulness, Tozer shows us that "the essential oneness of all the attributes soon become apparent" and that "His immutability presupposes His faithfulness. If He is unchanging, it follows that He could not be unfaithful, since that would require Him to change." Tozer is relating the fact that "all of God's acts are consistent with all of His attributes." With God, being and doing are always one. He writes, "We can hold a correct view of truth only by daring to believe everything God has said about Himself. It is a grave responsibility that a man takes upon himself when he seeks to edit out of God's self-revelation such features as he in his ignorance deems objectionable." Once again, these are words for our time.

## God's Goodness

Now as to the goodness of God, Tozer writes, "The goodness of God is that which disposes Him to be kind, cordial, benevolent, and full of good will toward men. He is tenderhearted and of quick sympathy and His unfailing attitude toward all moral beings is open, frank, and friendly. By His nature He is inclined to bestow blessedness and He takes holy pleasure in the happiness of His people." Could we only see this, we would begin to trust him more than we actually do. God indeed is benevolent. When we realize that there is no merit in human conduct—that if we turn to him in faith and repentance he promises to forgive us and to, as Psalm 103:12 states, remove our transgression "as far as the east is from the west"—how can we help but respond in humility and gratitude to such goodness? As Tozer observed, how can we fail to "believe that we dwell under a friendly sky"? We must recognize that the "God of heaven, though exalted in power and majesty, is eager to be friends with us." All of our rebellion ultimately stems from failing to understand that God is truly good, for if we really grasped that truth, we would not go our own way.

God's goodness is most evident in his sending of his Son to provide our means of salvation. Speaking of Jesus, Tozer writes, "From Him we learn how God acts toward people. The hypocritical, the basically insincere, will find Him cold and aloof, as they once found Jesus; but the penitent will find Him merciful; the self-condemned will find Him generous and kind. To the frightened He is friendly, to the poor in spirit He is forgiving, to the ignorant, considerate; to the weak, gentle; to the stranger, hospitable." Yet he admonishes, "If we would be welcomed as the Prodigal was, we must come as the Prodigal came." Of course, this requires the response of repentance and faith as well as submission to God's will.

## God's Justice

The necessity of Christ's incarnation is understood only in light of the justice of God. In speaking of God's justice, Tozer emphasizes that "all God's reasons come from within His uncreated being." Justice is the way God is, and he "is never at cross-purposes with Himself." He continues, "Redemptive theology teaches that mercy does not become effective toward a man until justice has done its work. The just penalty for sin was exacted when Christ our Substitute died for us on the cross." He is saying that this justice of God "stands forever against the sinner in utter severity. The vague and tenuous hope that God is too kind to punish the ungodly has become a deadly opiate for the consciences of millions. It hushes their fears and allows them to practice all pleasant forms of inquiry while death draws every day nearer and the command to repent goes unregarded."

## God's Mercy

The statement that God stands in judgment of sin is not well received by most people. It goes contrary to the grain of our own time, where we suppose God is a kind of benighted grandfather who dotes over us. In the chapter titled "The Mercy of God," Tozer writes, "We who earned banishment shall earn communion; we who deserve the pain of hell shall know the bliss of heaven." He adds that "as judgment is God's justice confronting moral inequity, so mercy is the goodness of God confronting human suffering and guilt."

## God's Grace

Tozer speaks of the grace of God and writes, "Grace is the good pleasure of God that inclines Him to bestow benefits on the undeserving." Indeed, that is a very good definition of grace. Tozer then goes on to declare, "No one was ever saved other than by grace, from Abel to the present moment. Since man was banished from the eastward garden, none has ever returned to the divine favor except through the sheer goodness of God. Wherever grace found any man it was always by Jesus Christ."

When people ask me about those who have never heard

the gospel, I respond that the *basis* for salvation through all ages and all places is always the same; it is the death and resurrection of Christ. The *means* of salvation is through faith. The *object* of that faith is God; but the *content* of that faith will depend on what revelation a person has received. Yet at the end of the day, it will be by grace through faith; it cannot be otherwise, because if otherwise, then Christ died needlessly. This is a truth Paul so clearly states in Galatians 2:21: "I do not nullify the grace of God, for if righteousness comes through the Law, then Christ died needlessly." There are essentially only two kinds of people in the world: those who seek God and those who seek to avoid him. Both will find what they seek in the end.

## God's Love

One of my favorite Tozer prayers appears at the opening of the chapter titled "The Love of God." Tozer prays,

> We are sure that there is in us nothing that could attract the love of One as holy and as just as Thou art. Yet Thou hast declared Thine unchanging love for us in Jesus Christ. If nothing in us can win Thy love, nothing in the universe can prevent Thee from loving us. Thy love is uncaused and undeserved. Thou art Thyself the reason for the love wherewith we are loved. Help us to believe the intensity, the eternity of the love that has found us. Then love will cast out fear; and our troubled hearts will be at peace, trusting not in what we are but in what Thou hast declared Thyself to be.

He also describes how "from God's other known attributes we may learn much about His love; . . . because He is eternal, His love can have no end; because He is infinite, He has no limit; because He is holy, it is the quintessence of all spotless purity; because He is immense, His love is an incomprehensibly vast, bottomless, shoreless sea before which we kneel in joyful silence and from which the loftiest eloquence retreats confused and abashed." Thus his love is "uncaused and undeserved"; he loves us simply because he chooses to love. He loved us so much that he did not spare his own Son, but rather sent him to satisfy the penalty justice required. God's love is indeed "incomprehensibly vast"!

Continuing on the theme of the love of God, Tozer speaks of God's benevolence, which literally means goodwill. He speaks of the fact that "God's love tells us that He is friendly." He speaks of God's love as "an emotional identification" and that "God takes pleasure in the object of His love." This then becomes an exploration of the pleasure of God as Tozer says, "God's work of creation was done to musical accompaniment," and he uses this imagery of love and of music and ties them together. He writes,

> Music is both an expression and a source of pleasure, and the pleasure that is purest and nearest to God is the pleasure of love. Hell is a place of no pleasure because there is no love there. Heaven is full of music because it is the place where the pleasures of holy love abound. Earth is the place where the pleasures of love are mixed with pain, for sin is here, and hate and ill will. In such a world as ours love must sometimes suffer, as Christ suffered in giving

Himself for His own. But we have the certain promise that the causes of sorrow will finally be abolished and the new race enjoys forever a world of selfless, perfect love.

## God's Holiness

Near the end of the book, Tozer includes a chapter titled "The Holiness of God," and in that section he writes, "Until we have seen ourselves as God sees us, we are not likely to be much disturbed over conditions around us as long as they do not get so far out of hand as to threaten our comfortable way of life. We have learned to live with unholiness and have come to look upon it as the natural and expected thing."

Tozer is quite right in describing that reality: "Holy is the way God is. To be holy He does not conform to a standard. He is that standard. He is absolutely holy with an infinite, incomprehensible fullness of purity that is incapable of being other than it is. Because He is holy, all His attributes are holy; that is, whatever we think of as belonging to God must be thought of as holy. God is holy and He has made holiness the moral condition necessary to the health of His universe." Yet no person is capable of holiness. Tozer answers this riddle by saying, "Caught in this dilemma, what are we Christians to do? . . . We must hide our unholiness in the wounds of Christ as Moses hid himself in the cleft of the rock while the glory of God passed by. We must take refuge from God in God. Above all we must believe that God sees us perfect in His Son while He disciplines and chastens and purges us that we may be partakers of His holiness."

## God's Sovereignty

The next to the last chapter of this little book bears the title "The Sovereignty of God." Tozer begins this chapter with a strong assertion: "God's sovereignty is the attribute by which he rules His entire creation, and to be sovereign God must be all-knowing, all-powerful, and absolutely free." In other words, God's sovereignty encompasses those other attributes of his character. Yet this introduces a philosophical dilemma of sorts, for why would God permit things within his creation of which he cannot approve, namely, evil, suffering, and death? This is a dilemma Tozer terms "the riddle of permitted evil." And second, how can God permit man to exercise free will in opposition to his own? The popular answers to these issues have often amounted to attacks on either God's sovereignty or his goodness, the responses of many of the Enlightenment philosophers, for example. Such men asserted that either God was not powerful enough to maintain absolute control over his created universe, or God was not fully good and therefore tolerated evil and suffering.

Obviously these are inadequate responses, given Scripture's clear revelation of God's character. Tozer then offers his position on these difficult issues:

> God sovereignly decreed that man should be free to exercise moral choice, and man from the beginning has fulfilled that decree by making his choice between good and evil. When he chooses to do evil, he does not thereby countervail the sovereign will of God but fulfills it, inasmuch as the eternal decree decided not which choice the man should make but that he should be free

to make it. . . . Man's will is free because God is sovereign. A God less than sovereign could not bestow moral freedom upon His creatures. He would be afraid to do so.

Yet at the conclusion of this chapter, Tozer acknowledges that ultimately a full reconciliation of these issues, given our limited understanding, is impossible; they remain a mystery. However he reminds us that whether we understand or not, "God is moving with infinite wisdom and perfect precision of action."

## Acquaintance with God

The last chapter of this extraordinary work is called "The Open Secret," and here Tozer concludes with his advice for the modern church universal. He asserts that if we want to be vibrant Christians who influence our world for good, we must come to grips with the secret that is not a secret—there are no shortcuts to spiritual growth. Tozer condenses everything he has said down to one simple exhortation: "Acquaint thyself with God." He then goes on to emphasize that God is not utilitarian; he is not merely trying to command attention and complete an agenda. Rather, God desires to draw all men to himself. He then admits that "to know God is at once the easiest and the most difficult thing in the world. It is easy because the knowledge is not won by hard mental toil, but is something freely given. . . . But this knowledge is difficult because there are conditions to be met and the obstinate nature of fallen man does not take kindly to them."

Tozer concludes the book by identifying six of these conditions that we must follow if we desire to enter into the experiential, personal, and relational knowledge of the holy. The first is the forsaking of our sins. This is not an event; it is a process. As God continues to illuminate new realms and new areas, and as we respond, he is free to work in us and transform us. The second is that "there must be an utter committal of the whole life to Christ in faith." We must recognize Christ's sufficient atonement for our sin and commit ourselves in faith to his sufficiency. The third condition is that "there must be a reckoning of ourselves to have died unto sin and to be alive unto God in Christ Jesus, followed by a throwing open of the entire personality to the inflow of the Holy Spirit." Here Tozer reminds us that new life is found in Christ and that regeneration is the work of the Holy Spirit.

The fourth condition declares that "we must boldly repudiate the cheap values of the fallen world and become completely detached in spirit from everything that unbelieving men set their hearts upon." Truly, that is a challenging one. In essence, it is the New Testament declaration that we must live in the world and yet not be of the world. Tozer's fifth exhortation is to "practice that art of long and loving meditation upon the majesty of God." Today this has almost been abandoned. I would strongly encourage you to take time in your life for study, meditation on God's Word and character, and prayer. This is the only solid path to spiritual maturity. Finally, the sixth condition is "as the knowledge of God becomes more wonderful, greater service to our fellow man will become for us imperative." He tells us that the "God who gave all to us will continue to give all through us as we come to know Him better." In other words, our love of God should enhance our love of others and our concern for their souls.

I believe this is an excellent way for him to conclude this remarkable book—in the realization that God desires us to know him and that in this increasing knowledge, he gives us the capacity to become lovers and servants of others. We will enjoy the fullness of the realization that as we serve others created in his image, we are investing in eternity because those people will go on forever.

Lord of wonder and awe, when we consider the mysteries of your divine attributes of self-existence, self-sufficiency, eternality, infinitude, immutability, omniscience, wisdom, omnipotence, transcendence, omnipresence, faithfulness, goodness, justice, mercy, grace, love, holiness, and sovereignty, we marvel at the mystery and majesty of who you are. Grant us the grace of holy aspiration to know you more intimately and respond to you in greater trust and obedience. In the name of your Son. Amen.

# NOTES

# Pride and Prejudice

## Introduction

Great literature is a gateway to penetrating insights on the human condition. The character arc from blindness to clarity, fear to heroism, self-centeredness to other-centeredness reveals the concerns with which we must wrestle to become men and women of integrity and depth. *Pride and Prejudice* brilliantly portrays the need to develop mutual respect, sympathy, and concern; to allow pain and misunderstanding to forge growing character; and to learn that the quality of our lives is directly related to the quality of our commitments and esteem for others. While this is not an overtly Christian novel, it evinces the moral obligations that flow from a Christian worldview.

*Pride and Prejudice* is an enchanting classic of romantic comedy written by Jane Austen, whom many regard to be one of the greatest female novelists. It is typically considered the finest of her six novels, all of which were written between 1796 and 1817. Her incredible wit and moral insight, sense of style, and remarkable skill in character development ensure that her works will endure.

She began writing *Pride and Prejudice* in October 1796, before she was even twenty-one years old. She completed it in about ten months, by August 1797. Of her novels, this one seems the least didactic and likely the most consistently entertaining. It is a novel of the mind and heart, containing a minimum of plot action. Instead, the movements consist of seeing and saying, thinking and feeling, wondering and assessing, hoping and fearing, and conjecturing and interpreting.

The nineteenth-century critic Richard Whately observed Austen's skill "in the art of copying from nature as she really exists in the common walks of life and presenting to the reader, instead of the pleasant scenes of the imaginary world, a correct and striking representation of that which is daily taking place around him."

Like most of Jane Austen's works, this novel employs a narrative technique that involves conversational and indirect speech. This technique has been defined as the "free representation of a character's speech, by which one means not words actually spoken by a character, but the words that typify the character's thoughts, or the way the character would think or speak if she thought or spoke." This technique invites the reader to follow the events that take place from the viewpoint of the central character, Elizabeth, share her prejudices and misapprehensions, and experience surprise along with her when events prove her perceptions wrong. In this way, we are caught within Elizabeth's misunderstandings and learn as she learns. This innovative technique of a limited omniscient point of view, coupled with Austen's rich social commentary and sense of irony, has earned her a place as one of the most beloved and widely read writers in English literature.

Jane Austen was influenced by the originators of the English novel, particularly Samuel Richardson and Henry Fielding. By combining the outward narrative (as in the manner of Fielding) with the inner workings behind that narrative (in the manner of Richardson) she moves us closer to the modern novel.

Jane Austen lived from 1775 to 1817; her parents, George and Cassandra, were members of prominent gentry families. Her father served as the rector of Anglican parishes in and around Steventon, Hampshire. There were eight children in the Austen family. In addition to six brothers, Jane had one sister—Cassandra—who was her closest friend and confidante throughout her life.

Although Jane and her sister briefly spent time in a boarding school, most of Jane's education was acquired by reading books, and she was guided by her father and two of her brothers—James and Henry—in this process. She remained in her parents' home into adulthood and engaged in a variety of family and social activities that were common to the period. These included playing the pianoforte, dancing, reading, and sewing; regular church attendance was also a significant part of her life.

Over the years as she was growing up, her family creatively staged a series of plays, and it may have been through these plays, particularly the comedies, that she developed her own comedic and satirical gifts. Jane began writing what is now known as her *juvenilia* between 1787 and 1793. This consisted of a variety of stories, poems, and plays, largely of a satirical nature and written predominantly for the amusement of her family.

Austen wrote a novella called *Love and Friendship* in 1789 and then another, which she called *Lady Susan*, in 1795. This second novella was a cynical work about a woman who used her superior intelligence and charm to manipulate and outwit others. It was during this period that she determined to become a professional writer. Her first full-length novel was titled *Elinor and Marianne*, and like her other writings, she read it serially to her family.

At the age of twenty, Austen spent considerable time with a young man named Tom Lefroy, the nephew of one of her neighbors in Steventon. His family put a stop to that potential romance when they sent Tom away, since neither of them was in a financial position to marry. It is likely that this experience may have inspired some of the material for her later books, including *Pride and Prejudice*.

Austen completed a second full-length novel called *First Impressions* in 1797. This work was later retitled *Pride and Prejudice*. The fact that she wrote this enduring literary classic at the age of only twenty-one underscores her remarkable literary ability. Her father sought to get *First Impressions* published but was rebuffed by the publisher.

Jane then returned to her work on *Elinor and Marianne*, revising it until it became the predecessor to her novel *Sense and Sensibility*. In 1799 she completed a satire of the popular gothic novel genre. She originally titled the work *Susan* and then later changed it to *Northanger Abbey*.

Late in 1800 the Reverend Austen retired from his parish ministry and moved the family to Bath. This move from the only home Jane had ever known was profoundly disturbing to her, and her productivity during these years in Bath greatly diminished.

Two years after the move, Jane received her only proposal of marriage. Harris Bigg-Wither was a friend of the family, and his resources would have been advantageous for Jane and enabled her to provide greater financial stability for her parents and sister. She initially accepted his proposal but then withdrew her acceptance, realizing that marriage without affection would have been a serious mistake.

Around that same time she began a new novel called *The Watsons* but stopped work on it when her father died in 1805. His death put Jane, her mother, and her sister in a precarious financial position that required the assistance of Jane's brothers. In 1809 Jane's brother Edward invited his mother and sisters to move to a cottage in Chawton that was part of his estate. This gave them a quiet and more stable life. It was at Chawton that Jane's literary career began to flourish.

Her novel *Sense and Sensibility* was published in 1811, and this was soon followed by the publication of *Pride and Prejudice* in 1813. Both of these novels enjoyed favorable reviews and sold well. The publication of *Mansfield Park* followed in 1814. Growing audiences admired Austen's works, including the prince regent, who even invited her to his residence in London.

Austen's next novel, *Emma*, was published in 1815, followed by *Persuasion*, in 1816. It was in this year that she began to suffer from a chronic illness, possibly Addison's disease or Hodgkin's lymphoma. Her physical condition gradually deteriorated. Although she began a novel called *The Brothers*, she was unable to complete it before her death in 1817 at the age of forty-one.

Her novel *Persuasion* was published posthumously in 1817 and sold as a set along with *Northanger Abbey*. For a time, Austen's book sales declined, and some of her books went out of print for a number of years until they were re-published in a set in 1833. Since that time her six novels have been continuously in print.

Her first works were published anonymously, but her brother Henry wrote a biographical note after Jane's death in 1817 that revealed her authorship of those earlier novels. Henry's biographical sketch of his sister was first published as a preface to the posthumous volume that contained *Persuasion* and *Northanger Abbey*. In this biographical note, he underscored the profound influence of their father and wrote, "Being not only a profound scholar, but possessing a most exquisite taste in every species of literature, is it not wonderful that his daughter, Jane, should at a very early age become sensible to the charms and style of the enthusiastic cultivation of her own language?" Her brother went on to write, "If there be an opinion current in the world that per-fect placidity of temper is not reconcilable to the most lively imagination, and the keenest relish for wit, such an opinion will be rejected forever by those who have the happiness of knowing the authoress of the following works."

Henry then described his sister with these words: "She was tranquil without reserve or stiffness and communicative without intrusion or self-sufficiency. She became an authoress entirely from taste and inclination; neither the hope of fame or profit mixed with her early motives. Most of her works as before observed were composed many years previous to their publication." Near the end of his biographical note, Henry added these important words: "One trait only remains to be touched on; it makes all others unimportant. She was thoroughly religious and devout, fearful of giving offense to God, and incapable of feeling it towards any fellow creature. On serious subjects she was well-instructed, both by reading and meditation, and her opinions accorded strictly with those of our established church." A letter Jane had written in 1814 to friend Fannie Knight seems to affirm her brother's assessments of her religious beliefs. In it, Jane confided, "I am by no means convinced that we ought not all of us to be evangelicals and I am at least persuaded that they who are so from reason and feeling must be happiest and safest."

Jane Austen's writings originally received only a few published reviews, but they were largely favorable. One of these was from the popular novelist Sir Walter Scott, who praised Austen's realism. Another prominent reviewer was Richard Whately, who extolled the dramatic quality of her novels. During the early nineteenth century, her writings were admired by only a small literary elite; she never attained the popular status enjoyed by Charles Dickens or George Eliot.

When her nephew James Edward Austen wrote a memoir of Jane Austen in 1860, however, her novels began to reach a wider audience. Popular illustrated editions of her works were published in the 1880s, and it was at this time that the first books of literary criticism of Austen were published. In the early twentieth century, her novels became a subject for academic study. Because of her narrative style and depth, Austen became recognized as one of the greatest writers of English fiction. Many critics admired her satire and her elevation of the status of women. Her works have enjoyed a surge in popular appreciation in recent years with their adaptation into film and television dramatizations, and numerous books and scripts have used updated versions of Austen's story lines.

As noted earlier, *First Impressions* was Jane Austen's original title for what later became *Pride and Prejudice*. She was encouraged by the publication of *Sense and Sensibility* to revise *First Impressions* and resubmit it for publication. Since that title had been recently used in both a novel and a play, she changed it to *Pride and Prejudice*, which was a common expression in her time. Unfortunately, her decision to accept a one-time payment from a publisher instead of royalties proved to be a financial mistake, since *Pride and Prejudice* sold much better than anticipated.

## Overview of the Plot

Austen's novel is set in the English countryside near a village roughly thirty miles from London. It introduces the Bennet family of Longbourn and the five unmarried Bennet daughters. Mrs. Bennet is intent on seeing her daughters married off to wealthy men. The satirical opening sentence sets the tone and theme of the entire novel: "It is a truth universally acknowledged, that a single man in possession of a good fortune must be in want of a wife."

When Mr. Bingley, an attractive, wealthy, and young London bachelor, leases nearby Netherfield Park, Mrs. Bennet is delirious with joy at the prospect of introducing her daughters to him. She immediately urges her husband to visit him, and through a series of humorous events, Mr. Bingley soon falls in love with Jane, the eldest of the five Bennet daughters.

However his friend, the wealthy and aristocratic Mr. Darcy, disapproves of Bingley's choice. Darcy considers the Bennet family to be socially inferior, and he plots with Bingley's sisters to separate the lovers. Meanwhile, Darcy himself is finding it hard to ignore his own increasing attraction to one of Jane's younger sisters, the vivacious Elizabeth. Elizabeth, however, develops prejudices against Darcy because he appears to be proud and conceited. Her prejudice grows when she later suspects his interference has torn Jane and Bingley apart. She is again outraged when she hears that Darcy has mistreated her new friend, George Wickham. Wickham informs her that Darcy denied him the inheritance promised him by Darcy's father, who was Wickham's godfather. For a brief time, Wickham courts Elizabeth, and his good looks, charming manners, and tragic story of injustice at the hand of Darcy win her sympathy and deepen her prejudice against Darcy.

Another complication in the plot involves the entailment of the Bennet estate. Because Mr. Bennet has no son, upon his death, his estate will be inherited by his nearest male relative, in this case an estranged nephew by the name of Mr. Collins. Collins is a pompous, young clergyman who has secured a comfortable income as a private parish minister to Mr. Darcy's aunt, Lady Catherine de Bourg. Lady de Bourg has commanded Mr. Collins to find a suitable wife, and so he has obediently traveled to Longbourn to seek a wife from among his cousins, believing their economic necessity (the entailment) will prompt a speedy acceptance to a proposal.

He is initially interested in Jane, but Mrs. Bennet quickly steers him away from her to Elizabeth. Without hesitation, he changes his affections and proposes to Elizabeth, who rejects him even though the marriage would keep Longbourn in her immediate family. Just days later, Mr. Collins proposes again and, this time, wins the acceptance of Elizabeth's best friend, Charlotte Lucas, a plain young woman of limited financial resources. She agrees to marry Collins merely to escape the shame of spinsterhood.

The story also interweaves several subplots. One of these occurs when Elizabeth visits Charlotte, who has since become Mrs. Collins, at the parsonage on Rosings Estate. While she is there, Mr. Darcy visits his aunt, Lady Catherine. Since she is also Mr. Collins's patron, Darcy and Elizabeth interact frequently. This leads to Darcy's proposal of marriage to her, when he admits, with more honesty than tact, that he is proposing against his better judgment. She angrily rejects him and accuses him of destroying Jane's happiness and Wickham's legitimate prospects.

Her response catches Darcy by surprise and prompts an earnest letter from him in which he provides information relevant to both her accusations. First, he acknowledges that he did interfere with Jane and Bingley, but only because he observed no evidence that Jane actually loved Bingley. He claims that he wanted only to save his friend from an unhappy marriage. Second, he explains that Wickham *did* receive his promised inheritance and more, but he squandered the money on gambling, drinking, and self-indulgences. When Darcy subsequently refused to give him further financial aid, he attempted to seduce and elope with Darcy's sixteen-year-old sister, Georgiana. Fortunately, the plot was discovered and the marriage prevented, but not without emotional harm to Georgiana.

Elizabeth is inclined to believe Darcy's explanations, and her prejudice against him gradually weakens. When she goes on a trip with her aunt and uncle, the Gardiners, they decide to tour Darcy's magnificent estate, Pemberley. In his absence they are shown through the house by his house-keeper, who praises him for his goodness and generosity and paints a very different picture of his character than the one Elizabeth had formed earlier. Unexpectedly, Darcy himself arrives. Elizabeth is mortified to be found there, but Darcy is full of courtesy to the Gardiners and very attentive to Elizabeth.

Yet soon after, bad news arrives from Longbourn: the youngest Bennet daughter, giddy and flirtatious sixteen-year-old Lydia, has run away with Wickham. Such a scandal is a disgrace to the whole family, and Elizabeth realizes with chagrin that now, just as her feelings toward Darcy have begun to change, any hope of a renewal of his proposal has been lost forever. Darcy, however, feels partially responsible for Lydia's elopement, thinking he should have warned the Bennets that Wickham had once tried the same tactic with his sister—besides, he is very much in love with Elizabeth. For her sake, he searches out the fugitive couple. He then arranges and pays for a legal marriage, settles Wickham's debts, and buys him a commission in the army. All this he does secretly, but Lydia accidentally reveals Darcy's part in her rescue, bringing Elizabeth to the realization that not only did she misjudge Darcy, but that he might still love her.

The book concludes happily as Bingley, with Darcy's encouragement, proposes to Jane and is accepted, and then

Darcy successfully offers his proposal again to Elizabeth. By this point, she has abandoned her prejudices, and he has subdued his pride.

## Characterizations

The novel opens with a conversation between the shallow and foolish Mrs. Bennet and her indifferent and sarcastic husband. When Mrs. Bennet informs Mr. Bennet that the nearby estate of Netherfield has been leased by a young man of large fortune, their conversation reveals much about the novel's central theme:

> Mr. Bennet: "What is his name?"
>
> Mrs. Bennet: "Bingley."
>
> Mr. Bennet: "Is he married or single?"
>
> Mrs. Bennet: "Oh, single, my dear, to be sure. A single man of large fortune . . . four or five thousand a year. What a fine thing for our girls."
>
> Mr. Bennet: "How so? How can it affect them?"
>
> Mrs. Bennet: "My dear Mr. Bennet, how can you be so tiresome? You must know that I am thinking of his marrying one of them."
>
> Mr. Bennet: "Is that his design in settling here?"
>
> Mrs. Bennet: "Design, nonsense! How can you talk so? But it is very likely that he may fall in love with one of them, and, therefore, you must visit him as soon as he comes."

Here Austen attacks a common impetus for marriage in her time period: financial advancement. The novel's opening line, as already noted, reveals her critique quite clearly: "It is a truth universally acknowledged that a single man in possession of a good fortune must be in want of a wife." Austen's sardonic declaration that money, not love, motivates many unsuitable marriages sets the tone for her novel's social criticisms. It also spurs the reader to reflect on what considerations should precede the decision to marry. From the very beginning of her novel, Austen labors to depict the true purpose of marriage and family, and she does so by providing positive and negative examples for the reader to examine.

Serving in a negative capacity, Elizabeth's mother, Mrs. Bennet, is characterized by ill-judged officiousness, manipulative ploys, and silly remarks. Her superficiality is always evident. For most of the plot, she loathes Mr. Darcy, yet when she discovers, near the end of the novel, that Elizabeth is going to marry him, she says, "Good gracious! Lord, bless me. Just think, Mr. Darcy. Who would have thought it? . . . How rich and how great you will be. What pin-money, what jewels, what carriages you will have. Jane's is nothing to it, nothing at all. I am so pleased, so happy. Such a charming man; so handsome, so tall. Oh, my dear Lizzy, pray apologize for my having disliked him so much before. I hope he will overlook it. Dear, dear Lizzy, a house in town, everything that is charming. Three daughters married. Ten thousand a year. Dear Lord, what will become of me? I shall go distracted." Here Austen emphasizes Mrs. Bennet's complete disregard for true happiness in marriage. She gives no thought to compatibility, respect, or affection. Instead she focuses solely on the material and social advantages marriage potentially provides.

By contrast, Austen portrays Elizabeth's father, Mr. Bennet, as much more sensible, yet he too serves as a negative example: "Mr. Bennet was so odd a mixture of quick parts, sarcastic humor, reserve, and caprice that the experience of three and twenty years had been insufficient to make his wife understand his character. Her mind was less difficult to develop. She was a woman of mean understanding, little information, and uncertain temper. When she was discontented, she fancied herself nervous. The business of her life was to get her daughters married. Its solace was visiting and news." While readers like Mr. Bennet more than they like his wife, he clearly possesses severe character flaws. Among these flaws is the fact that he employs his sarcastic wit at his wife's expense, often in the presence of their children. Elizabeth makes the unpleasant observation at one point in the novel that her father had long ago made the mistake of marrying for reasons other than love and then resigned himself to living with his choice:

> Her father, captivated by youth and beauty, and that appearance of good humor which youth and beauty generally give, had married a woman whose weak understanding and illiberal mind had very early in their marriage put an end to all real affection for her. Respect, esteem, and confidence had vanished forever; and all his view of domestic happiness were overthrown. . . . To his wife he was very little otherwise indebted than as her ignorance and folly had contributed to his amusement. This is not the sort of happiness which a man would in general wish to owe his wife. . . .

> Elizabeth, however, had never been blind to
> the impropriety of her father's behavior as a
> husband. She had always seen it with pain. . . .
> [She] endeavored to forget what she could not
> overlook, and to banish from her thoughts that
> continual breach of conjugal obligation and
> decorum which, in exposing his wife to the
> contempt of her own children, was so highly
> reprehensible.

With these observations, Austen levels a harsh criticism on Mr. Bennet. The reader pities him in his marital misery, yet his behavior is inexcusable. Although he has remained physically faithful, his contempt has infected their daughters as he has modeled disrespect and disregard for his wife in front of them. Elizabeth goes on to say that "she had never felt so strongly . . . the disadvantages that must attend the children of so unsuitable a marriage, nor ever been so fully aware of the evils arising from so ill-judged a direction of talents which rightly used might have at least have preserved the respectability of his daughters, even if incapable of enlarging the mind of his wife."

With this description of the Bennets' relationship and their individual personalities, Austen alludes to two of her central themes. First, marriage depends on mutual respect. Second, marriage affects society. While pre-Victorian society tended to degrade marriage into a mere social institution designed to provide for personal comfort, status, and security, Austen uses her novel to reassert its fundamental importance as the cornerstone of the family and society. Through her characters, she labors to show the benefits, personal *and* societal, of marriages based on mutual respect and the detriments of marriages motivated by superficial concerns.

For that reason, she includes Mr. Collins's humorous yet pathetic proposal of marriage to Elizabeth, who soundly refuses him, saying, "You could not make *me* happy, and I am convinced that I am the last woman in the world who would make *you* so." Elizabeth has apparently learned from observing her unhappy parents, and she wisely avoids a marriage that might tempt her to emulate her father's behavior. While her mother is outraged and cannot understand why Elizabeth would refuse a proposal, her father understands only too well. At Mrs. Bennet's ultimatum that she will never speak to Elizabeth again unless she accepts the proposal, her father responds, "An unhappy alternative is before you, Elizabeth. From this day you must be a stranger to one of your parents. Your mother will never see you again if you do not marry Mr. Collins; and I will never see you again if you do." Although he cannot salvage his own happiness, he can still play a role in promoting the happiness of his favorite daughter.

Yet Mr. Bennet's general aloofness and emotional distance prevent him from seeing the dangers his youngest daughters face. Sadly, he treats them with much of the same dismissiveness with which he regards their mother. Believing "[they] were hopeless of remedy" and contenting himself "with laughing at them, [he] would never exert himself to restrain the wild giddiness of his youngest daughters." His apathy and failure to lovingly discipline his children eventually result in much misfortune for them and the entire family.

Having abandoned his primary leadership role over his family, Mr. Bennet summarizes his life with these sad words: "For what do we live, but to make sport for our neighbors and laugh at them in our turn?" Mr. Bennet abdicates his roles as husband and father and, as a spectator, merely watches others play their roles. And while he is quick to observe various discrepancies or ridiculous mannerisms, Mr. Bennet refuses to assume the role of father and landowner. His escapism from social commitment and his withdrawal from family life are presented as serious faults in his character.

English literature scholar Alistair Duckworth has summarized the dysfunctional Bennet family in this way:

> Mr. Bennet's somewhat cynical irony, his wife's fixed concern to marry off her daughters, Jane's indiscriminate benevolence, Mary's pedantry, and the youngest sister's love of the military are all evident as too are Elizabeth's perceptiveness and special position. Elizabeth and her older sister, Jane, are allies in this novel. Their powers of conversation are considerable. They could describe an entertainment with accuracy, relate an anecdote with humor, and laugh at their acquaintance with spirit. The third sister, Mary, is socially inept. Although she has acquired knowledge and some accomplishments, she lacks discernment and compassion. The two youngest daughters, Kitty and Lydia, both lack education and sense. They seek attention, entertainment, and excitement. Lydia in particular contrasts the oldest Bennet daughters, for she is characterized by a complete lack of restraint or concern for the well-being of anyone but herself.

In addition to the Bennet family, Mr. Collins, Mr. Darcy, and several other characters serve to illuminate Austen's themes. Lady de Bourg illustrates the artificial divisions that exist within pre-Victorian aristocracy, and she also provides a sort of comic relief within the plot. Charlotte Lucas offers a glimpse into the perspective of many young women of the day, who would rather marry without love than face the loneliness and insecurity inherent in remaining single. George Wickham plays a vital role in the plot, first as a sympathetic character and later as a villain. Mr. Bingley and his sisters offer yet another glimpse into the English nobility and their attitudes, and finally the Gardners provide an example of a healthy marriage, based on mutual love and respect.

## Themes

Austen develops several primary themes in her novel, but the most obvious involves the title traits of pride and prejudice. While many characters exhibit facets of these vices, Elizabeth and Darcy clearly learn the most about their vulnerability in these areas. Through their mistakes, suffering, and growth, the reader acquires insight and applications for his or her own life.

It is evident that Elizabeth's first impression of Darcy is quite negative. She deems him aloof, proud, and condescending, particularly when he wounds her pride by referring to her appearance as "tolerable." Mrs. Bennet is equally disappointed in him and tells her husband that "Lizzy does not lose much by not suiting his fancy, for he is a most disagreeable, horrid man, not at all worth pleasing; so high and so conceited that there was no enduring him. He walked here; he walked there, fancying himself so great. . . . I quite detest the man."

Later Elizabeth tells her sister Mary that she could easily forgive Darcy's pride if he had not mortified hers, prompting Mary to make this observation concerning the matter of pride: "There are very few of us who do not cherish a feeling of self-complacency on this score of some quality or other, real or imaginary. Vanity and pride are different things, though the words are often used synonymously. A person may be proud without being vain. Pride relates more to our opinion of ourselves; while vanity to what we would have others think of us." Austen uses Elizabeth's injured pride, snap judgments of Darcy's character, and security in the affirmation of her friends and family to lay the groundwork for her errors in judgment and later her self-discovery and growth. At this point in the novel, Elizabeth is overconfident in her powers of discernment. This is evident in a conversation between her and Darcy, where he observes that "nothing is more deceitful . . . than the appearance of humility. It is often only carelessness of opinion and sometimes an indirect boast." With this statement, the author warns her reader of the inherent difficulty of discerning accurately between appearance and reality.

As the novel continues, Elizabeth's opinion of Darcy only worsens, especially when Wickham convincingly impugns his character, saying, "He can be a good companion if he thinks it is worth his while. Among those who are at all his equals of consequence he is a very different man from what he is to the less prosperous. His pride never deserts him; but with the rich he is liberal-minded, just, sincere, rational, honorable, and perhaps agreeable, allowing something for fortune and figure." Elizabeth unwisely accepts this assessment of Darcy's character without question.

She prides herself on her insights into the human condition, and she tells her sister Jane, "There are very few people whom I really love; and still fewer of whom I think well. The more I see of the world, the more am I dissatisfied with it. Every day confirms my belief of the inconstancy of all human characters and of the little dependence that can be placed on the appearance of either merit or sense." Here she reveals a dangerous cynicism and judgmentalism, qualities that lead her to draw faulty conclusions. In an earlier conversation with Elizabeth, Darcy had observed, "There is, I believe, in every disposition a tendency to some particular evil, a natural defect which not even the best education can overcome." To which Elizabeth had responded, "And your defect is the propensity to hate everybody." Darcy had then retorted, with a smile, "And yours is willfully to misunderstand them." This conversation makes it clear that both characters struggle with inordinate pride and judgmental tendencies, and ironically, they are even somewhat aware of those character weaknesses.

Later, Elizabeth's pride in her own abilities is abased when she discovers that her assessments of Darcy, as well as of Wickham, have been entirely wrong. She realizes that she has been blind, partial, prejudiced, and absurd: "How despicably have I acted," she cried. "I, who have prided myself in discernment; I, who have valued myself and my abilities, who has often disdained the candor of my sister and gratified my vanity in useless or blamable distrust; how humiliating is this discovery." Although this is one of the most painful lessons of her young life, it proves a pivotal point of growth in her character development.

Darcy's pride resurfaces as the novel progresses, for he finds himself resisting his growing affection for Elizabeth because of it. While he admires her, he regards her family as an embarrassment and her social status as inferior to his own, opinions he reveals in his proposal. Commenting on Darcy's misguided approach, Claudia L. Johnson comments: "So little is Darcy concerned with Elizabeth's happiness that he does not hesitate to inform her of the damage he is doing to his own self-consequence by proposing marriage to her in the first place—expressing his sense of her inferiority, of its being a degradation of the family obstacles, which judgment has always opposed to inclination." Johnson goes on to write, "Unless we acknowledge that Darcy's pride is a criminal assault on Elizabeth's happiness, we will not appreciate the profundity of his eventual transformation."

Elizabeth's existing prejudices compounded by Darcy's expressed reluctance to marry beneath his station lead her to indignantly reject his offer in the most certain of terms: "From the very beginning, from the first moment, I may almost say, of my acquaintance with you, your manners impressing me with the fullest belief of your arrogance and conceit, and your selfish disdain of the feelings of others, was such as to form that ground work of disapprobation on which succeeding events have built so immovable a dislike and I have not known you a month before I felt that you were the last man in the world whom I could ever be prevailed on to marry." Once again, however, intense emotional pain proves the catalyst for personal growth, for when Elizabeth angrily accuses Darcy of behaving in an ungentlemanly manner, he is cut to the quick. It is this accusation that prompts him not only to correct her wrongful judgments of him via a letter of explanation, but also to begin to scrutinize his attitudes and behavior.

This self-scrutiny is made evident near the end of the novel when Darcy tells Elizabeth: "What did you say of me that I did not deserve? For though your accusations were ill-founded, formed on mistaken premises, my behavior to you at the time had merited the severest reproof. It was unpardonable. I cannot think of it without abhorrence." Elizabeth responds, "We will not quarrel for the greater share of the blame. The conduct of neither, if strictly examined, would be irreproachable. But since then we have both, I hope, improved in civility." With these statements, Austen makes it clear that her characters have undergone a maturing process through suffering and self-examination.

In reference to the letter Darcy writes to refute Elizabeth's unfounded accusations, literary critic Susan Fraiman observes, "This is the point, the dead center on which the whole book turns. Darcy's botched proposal marks the nadir of his career after which, launched by his letter, he rises up from infamy in an arc that approaches apotheosis." *Apotheosis* is perhaps quite a strong term to describe Darcy's growth, for it seems to fall a bit short of glorification or deification, yet his transformation and genuine humility set him apart from most other men and make him admirable not only in Elizabeth's eyes but also in the reader's eyes.

Austen's novel also deals with characters who fail to recognize their character weaknesses. Mr. William Collins is such a character. He is the most comical character in the novel. Furthermore, he is pompous, boring, and sycophantic. Listen to this conversation between Mr. Bennet and

Mr. Collins where Mr. Bennet inquires, "It is happy for you to possess the talent of flattering with delicacy. May I ask whether these pleasing attentions proceed from the impulse of the moment, or are they the result of previous study?" To which Collins responds, "They arise chiefly from what is passing at the time. And though I sometimes amuse myself with suggesting and arranging, such little elegant compliments that may be adapted on ordinary occasions, I always wish to give them as unstudied an air as possible." His open admission that he deliberately seeks to flatter people of influence humorously reveals one aspect of his severely flawed character.

Austen then interjects, "Mr. Bennet's expectations were fully answered. His cousin was absurd as he had hoped. . . . Mr. Collins was not a sensible man and the deficiency of nature had been but little assisted by education or society. A fortunate chance had recommended him to Lady Catherine de Bourg when the living of Huntsford was vacant. And the respect which he felt for her high rank and his veneration for her as his patroness, mingling with a very good opinion of himself, of his authority as a clergyman, and his rights as a rector, made him altogether a mixture of pride and obsequiousness, self-importance, and humility."

A little later when Collins proposes to Elizabeth, claiming to be "run away" with his feelings, the narrator interjects, "The idea of Mr. Collins, with all his solemn composure being run away with by his feelings, made Elizabeth so near laughing that she could not use the short pause he allowed in any attempt to stop him farther and he continued." Not only does Mr. Collins *not* love Elizabeth, but his self-professed, threefold purpose for marrying is (1) to make himself happy,

(2) to set a good example for his parishioners, and (3) to please his patroness. Love for Elizabeth doesn't even make his top-three list.

Critic Dorothy Van Ghent makes this observation about Mr. Collins's elaborate but ineffectual proposal of marriage to Elizabeth: "Fancy syntax acts here, not as an expression of moral and intellectual refinement as Mr. Collins intends it to act, but as an expression of stupidity—the antithesis of that refinement. The elaborate language in which Mr. Collins gets himself fairly stuck is mimesis of an action of the soul that becomes self-dishonest through failure to know itself and that overrates itself at the expense of social context just as it overrates verbalism at the expense of meaning."

The comic effect of the situation heightens when Elizabeth declines his proposal, but Mr. Collins refuses to believe that she is serious. His pride and smug self-satisfaction lead him to assume that she is declining out of fashion, and it is only when she finally flees the room that he grasps the sincerity of her refusal. Austen then describes his reaction: "He was meditating in solitude on what had passed. He thought too well of himself to comprehend on what motive his cousin could refuse him. And though his pride was hurt, he suffered in no other way." Austen's emphasis on his self-interest relieves the reader of any sympathy that might be felt toward Mr. Collins and permits us to laugh at, and hopefully learn from, the clergyman's confusion over Elizabeth's adamant refusal.

Collins soon finds a willing marriage partner in Charlotte Lucas, however, whose philosophy of marriage differs greatly from Elizabeth's. Charlotte argues that "happiness in marriage is entirely a matter of chance. If the dispositions of the party are ever so well known to each other or ever so similar beforehand, it does not advance their felicity in the least. They always grow sufficiently unlike afterwards to have their share of vexation. It is better to know as little as possible of the defects of the person with whom you are to pass your life." This utilitarian approach makes her willing to accept Mr. Collins's offer. The narrator sums up her attitude this way:

> Mr. Collins, to be sure, was neither sensible nor agreeable. His society was irksome and his attachment to her must be imaginary. But still, he would be her husband. Without thinking highly of men or of matrimony, marriage had always been her object. It was the only honorable provision for well-educated young women of small fortune; and however uncertain of giving happiness must be their pleasantest preservative from want. This preservative she had now obtained and at the age of twenty-seven without having ever been handsome, she felt all the good luck of it.

With this sad assessment of Collins's flawed character, Austen communicates the misery to which Charlotte has likely doomed herself by committing to a loveless marriage of convenience.

Mr. Collins is not completely without passion, however. His fawning adulation of Lady Catherine is only too apparent: "The power of displaying the grandeur of his patroness to his wondering visitors, and of letting them see her civility towards himself and his wife was exactly what he wished for. And that an opportunity for doing it should be given so soon was such an instance of Lady Catherine's condescension as he knew not how to admire enough." Mr. Collins's inordinate pride leads him to value status and social connections over genuine relationships.

Another pompous character whose pride is never amended is the aforementioned Lady Catherine de Bourg. Her greatest delight is found in reminding those around her of their social inferiority. The narrator describes this scene after a dinner at Lady Catherine's estate: "When the ladies returned to the drawing room there was little to be done but to hear Lady Catherine talk, which she did without any intermission until the coffee came in, delivering her opinion on every subject in so decisive a manner as proved she was not used to having her judgment controverted." While she is wealthy and aristocratic, Lady Catherine reveals herself to be boorish, rude, condescending, and arrogant—a fact that embarrasses Darcy. He recognizes the silliness of his aunt, and seems to understand that despite her wealth and "breeding," she behaves no better than Elizabeth's foolish mother.

One of the most memorable incidents of the novel occurs when Lady de Bourg visits Longbourn to interrogate Elizabeth about her relationship with Darcy. As his aunt, she has unilaterally decided that he must marry her meek, sickly daughter; but when she hears rumors that Darcy is engaged to Elizabeth, she immediately travels to Longbourn to dissuade Elizabeth from such a marriage. Her unmerited outrage is comical as she explains her daughter's claim to Darcy:

> The engagement between them is of a peculiar kind. From their infancy they have been intended for each other. It was the favorite wish of his mother as well as of hers. While in their cradles we planned the union and now at the moment when the wishes of both

sisters be accomplished in their marriage, to
be prevented by a young woman of inferior
birth and of no importance in the world and
wholly unallied to the family, do you pay no
regard to the wishes of his friends to his tacit
engagement with Miss de Bourg? Or are you
lost to every feeling of propriety and delicacy?
Have you not heard me say that from his earli-
est hours he was destined for his cousin?

As the critic Nina Auerbach observes, "Lady Catherine's authority is not inherent, but derived in arbitrary and misplaced
fashion from accidents and contrivances outside herself. She
is a pastiche of external pretensions, an embodiment of that
power without selfhood that threatens to make all authority
ridiculous."

As she addresses issues of pride, prejudice, selfishness,
and superficiality, Austen also counters them by illustrat-
ing the importance of mutual respect to a happy, healthy
relationship. She does this, in part, through the example of
the Gardners and through the eventual relationship between
Darcy and Elizabeth.

The Gardners' marriage provides an example of the benefits of marrying suitably. They enjoy each other's company,
cooperate to raise happy and sensible children, and exert a
positive influence on others. Both also involve themselves in
the lives of their beloved nieces, providing the guidance and
diplomacy that the girls' own parents fail to provide.

When Elizabeth begins to voice cynicism about men
and romance, saying, "Stupid men are the only ones worth
knowing," her aunt wisely cautions, "Take care, Lizzy;
that speech savours strongly of disappointment." She also

cautions Elizabeth to take care in forming her judgments of others, prodding her to consider character carefully before establishing a firm opinion.

Mr. and Mrs. Gardner both make efforts to build constructive relationships with their nieces. They bring the disappointed Jane back to London with them after Bingley discontinues his courtship. They take Elizabeth with them on a short vacation to rural England. Mr. Gardner pursues young Lydia when she elopes with Wickham, and both Gardners lovingly attempt to help her recognize the error of her actions and the pain she has caused others.

Through the Gardners' marriage, Austen offers the novel's only example of an ideal marriage. Their marriage is characterized by respect, affection, fidelity, and benevolence. They bring out the best in each other and those around them. In short, the Gardners help Elizabeth, and the reader, to aspire to something better than what Charlotte tolerates or the Bennets endure.

The significance of this example becomes evident as Austen develops the relationship between Darcy and Elizabeth. In slow degrees they begin to recognize not only their individual failings but also each other's strengths. Darcy admires Elizabeth's independent mind, loyalty to family, and exuberance. Elizabeth grows to admire Darcy's consistency, generosity, sincerity, and selflessness. As they learn more about each other, genuine affection and respect overwhelm their wounded pride and previous prejudices. When they finally reconcile at the end of the novel, their mutual respect is evident. Darcy has labored to improve Elizabeth's opinion of him, and Elizabeth is equally eager to prove that she has changed for the better. A grateful Darcy proclaims to Elizabeth, "Dearest, loveliest Elizabeth! What do I not owe you! You taught me a lesson, hard indeed at first, but most advantageous. By you I was properly humbled. . . . You showed me how insufficient were all my pretensions to please a woman worthy of being pleased." Elizabeth likewise expresses remorse over her previous attitudes and behavior and reveals a maturity and humility that were previously lacking.

Austen reiterates respect as the central pillar of marriage in a scene between Elizabeth and her father. Darcy has since requested permission to marry her, and Mr. Bennet calls Elizabeth in to question her about her feelings on the issue. He earnestly asks, "Lizzy, what are you doing? Are you out of your senses, to be accepting this man? Have not you always hated him? . . . He is rich, to be sure, and you may have more fine clothes and fine carriages than Jane. But will they make you happy?"

He then goes on to make an impassioned plea: "I know that you could be neither happy nor respectable, unless you truly esteemed your husband, unless you looked up to him as a superior. Your lively talents would place you in the greatest danger in an unequal marriage. You could scarcely escape discredit and misery. My child, let me not have the grief of seeing *you* unable to respect your partner in life. You know not what you are about" (italics original).

This conversation reveals the heart of a man who has learned much from his errors and suffering. His own unequal marriage and inability to respect his spouse have led him to use his intellect destructively—to sarcastically tear down rather than build up his life partner. He recognizes the danger for his beloved daughter and seeks to make her aware of the danger she potentially faces.

Although the reader understands that Elizabeth is *not* making a marital mistake, Austen uses this scene to reiterate her central theme: respect is the basis of all healthy relationships, and pride and prejudice develop when respect is lacking. In a letter of gratitude from Elizabeth to her aunt Gardner, Austen includes one final image to convey the value of true love and mutual respect when Elizabeth writes, "I am the happiest creature in the world. . . . I am happier even than Jane; she only smiles, I laugh." While their unequal marriages condemn Mr. Bennet and Charlotte Lucas-Collins to a lifetime of only laughing *at* their spouses, Elizabeth anticipates a life of love and growth as she laughs *with* her spouse—a significant contrast.

## Conclusion

*Pride and Prejudice* marks a critical point in Jane Austen's career insofar as it reveals her insightful regard of social and moral realities. While the setting and the social circumstances of this novel are indeed restricted, Austen evinces an artistic mastery within these limited materials and range. The sphere of this novel is primarily limited to a few families in a country village. There is little interest in organized society as a whole and no real interest for the great social and political problems being debated in her day. Donald Gray, editor of the Norton Critical Edition of our present book, observes: "*Pride and Prejudice*, like her other novels, is a story about people who learn or who fail to learn; how to be, do, and recognize good in the ordinary passages of lives that would be unremarkable if Austen had not made it clear that a kind of moral salvation depends upon what Elizabeth and Darcy make of themselves by learning about one another." Austen proves herself capable of looking with the greatest insight into human character, foibles, and dispositions and understanding why people act as they do and where misunderstandings arise.

Part of Austen's genius is her ability to contemplate struggles, vices, and virtues in a kindly and humorous manner. Alistair Duckworth observes that

> the language base of the Austen novel gives us the limiting conditions of the culture. Somehow, using this language of inquisitiveness and calculation and materialism, a language common to the most admirable characters as well as to the basest characters in the book, the spiritually creative persons will have to form their destinies. Fortunately, for the drama of the Austen novel, there is this difficulty of the single, materialistic language, for drama subsists on difficulty. Within the sterile confines of public consumptions, the Austen protagonists find with difficulty the fertility of honest and intelligent individual feeling.

Critic D. W. Harding comments that "Austen's books are as she meant them to be, read and enjoyed by precisely the sort of people whom she disliked. She is a literary classic of the society which attitudes like hers, held widely enough, would undermine. Through her skillful and playful use of caricature, she was capable of finding a mode of existence for her very critical attitudes, which she was capable of keeping on reasonably good terms with the associates of her everyday life."

The late English scholar Tony Tanner makes this insightful observation: "One of the gratifications of the book is that Elizabeth and Darcy seem to demonstrate that it is still possible for individuals to make new connections in defiance of society. That there is perhaps a fairytale touch to their total felicity at the conclusion of the dream world of Pemberley would not discourage us from recognizing the importance of holding onto the possibility as one which is essential to a healthy society; that is to say, a society in which the individual can experience freedom as well as commitment."

As all these critics have observed, there is a delicate balance in this book. Austen successfully criticizes the mores and attitudes of her culture, but her criticisms are mollified by her use of humor and her affirmations of the goodness that remains a part of human nature. Furthermore, she asserts the value of a social structure, even one that is flawed. Elizabeth exemplifies a discerning and intelligent young woman who, although enmeshed in a complex web of social expectations and values, thrives. Austen affirms the fact that the individual is really not able to find a true identity without the context of some kind of social environment.

There are a depth and an attractiveness in this novel that revel in the tension between the individual and society as a whole. Both Darcy and Elizabeth must learn to make important concessions. Elizabeth must come to understand that individualism needs to be bounded by social limits, whereas Darcy must realize that tradition without individual energy and options is something that is really empty and meaningless. There is a satisfactory conclusion when the relationship between the individual and society is balanced and both are affirmed.

*Pride and Prejudice* stresses the need for reconciliation. Dorothy Van Ghent puts it this way: "The incongruities between savage impulses and the civilized conventions, in which they are buried, between utility and morality, are reconciled in this symbolic act of a marriage which society itself, bent on useful marriages, has paradoxically done everything to prevent." Rightly, the next to last word in the book is the word *uniting*.

This novel is rich in intertwining ironies and personal discovery. The terms *pride* and *prejudice* are interchangeably applicable to both the hero and the heroine; as we see Elizabeth's prejudice modified, so we see Darcy's pride humbled. The lessons that Darcy and Elizabeth need to learn, however, are different. Darcy's pride in the superiority of his behavior leads to his prejudicial views; and Elizabeth's prejudice stems from an unjustifiable pride in the infallibility of her own perception. Thus, both characters, really, illustrate the two sides of pride and prejudice. While Elizabeth has prided herself throughout this novel in her discriminatory powers and her ability to discern character, the irony at the end is her discovery that her discernment is *not* infallible and that she is not always correct in her appraisals of individuals or human nature. Likewise, Darcy learns that his behavior at times has been ungentlemanly, and he strives to amend it.

Twenty-first-century readers who first encounter this novel may find it slow, and perhaps even tedious, because it deals with ideas more than actions. But the reader who perseveres will discover that it contains tremendous depth and that the ideas and discoveries presented in the novel are actually quite exciting and exhilarating.

Austen's own complex personality is quite evident in her heroine, Elizabeth. With regard to this, critic Marvin Mudrick notes, "[Elizabeth's] continual mistake is to ignore or set aside as uninfluential the social context. It is a question not merely of individuals and marriage, but individuals and marriage in an acquisitive society. Elizabeth expects nothing except comfort or amusement from simplicity, but she likes to believe that complexity means a categorically free will without social distortion or qualifications."

The novel illustrates that there are multiple ways of approaching a person's character, and this is particularly evident in Elizabeth's growing grasp of the character of Darcy. Elizabeth's penchant for cynicism is balanced by her older sister, Jane. Jane understands that to view the world in a cold manner is to be neither perceptive nor superior—nor is it safe from being wrong; it is to be irresponsible, and it is to abandon the difficulties of trust for the finality of easy generalization. Unlike her cynically objective father, Elizabeth must learn to gain a real sympathy for others, to use her quick mind, and to reach for hope and suggestive meanings rather than just being distant and ironic.

Critic Margaret Oliphant has summarized Austen's perspective on the society in which she lived:

> It is the soft and silent disbelief of a spectator who has to look at a great many things without showing any outward discomposure, and who has learned to give up any moral classification of social sins and to place them instead on the level of absurdities. She is not surprised or offended, much less horror stricken or indignant, when her people show vulgar or mean

traits of character, when they demonstrate how self-absorbed they are, or even when they fall into those social cruelties which selfish and stupid people are so often guilty of; not without intention, but yet without the power of realizing half the pain they inflict. She stands by and looks on, and gives a soft, half-smile, and tells the story with an exquisite sense of its ridiculous side and finds stinging, yet soft-voiced contempt for the actors in it. The attitude is not one of contempt, but of tolerance and patience tempered with a kind of tone of general disbelief—indeed, of amusement about those humorous components of humanity that may appear to be quaint, but yet there is a lovable and meaningful side to them.

In 1821 Richard Whately commented on Austen's careful and subtle use of Christian and moral themes. He wrote that "Miss Austen has the merit, in our judgment, most essential to being evidently a Christian writer; a merit that is much enhanced both on the score of good taste and of practical utility, by her religion being not at all obtrusive." Whately went on to write that "the moral lessons, also, of this lady's novels, though clearly and impressively conveyed, are not offensively put forward, but spring incidentally from the circumstances of the story. They are not forced upon the reader, but he is left to collect them, though without any difficulty, for himself. Hers is that unpretending kind of instruction which is furnished by real life and certainly no author has ever conformed more closely to real life as well as in the incidents, as in the characters, and the descriptions."

Austen also wrote a number of prayers, and these reveal that a disposition to think well of self and ill of others contradicts what she conceived to be the Christian's duty. In one of her prayers she wrote, "Incline us, O God, to think humbly of ourselves, to be severe only in the examination of our own conduct, to consider our fellow creatures with kindness, and to judge of all they say and do with that charity which we would desire of them ourselves." It is this sort of charity, or unconditional love, that *Pride and Prejudice* associates with Elizabeth's older sister, Jane, a charity that Elizabeth herself learns through pain and error. Yet critic Marilyn Butler adds this very important insight:

> We would not exchange Elizabeth's intelligence for Jane's innocence, or Darcy's constancy for Bingley's pliancy, even though the faults of the central couple lead them into worse moral error. But in fact, the author does not want us to. It is clear that her view of the truly Christian character blends the best qualities of all four. Elizabeth and Darcy take a properly pessimistic view of human liability to error. And rightly applied, their perceptiveness will be a great moral quality for Jane Austen insists that the scrupulous self-knowledge which she prizes is the product of their kind of skeptical intelligence.

One of the great contributions of this novel is that it poignantly illustrates the significance of love and charity in a society in which money, marriage, and social status have become the measure of all morality. Austen's writings also demonstrate the importance of environment and upbringing in the development of young people's character and moral understanding, and *Pride and Prejudice* in particular emphasizes a central truth in Christian living—namely, that real love is transformative and capable of enduring all things.

Lord of love, light, and life, teach us to treasure the relationships that you have entrusted to us. By your grace and power, let us grow in other-centered commitment, sympathy, and respect for the people in our lives. May we learn to examine ourselves rightly so that we will love others well. We ask these things in Jesus' name. Amen.

# NOTES

# The Love of God

## Introduction

A number of years ago, a series of books called Classics of Faith and Devotion was published. The series focused on the writings of a number of church leaders from across the centuries, one of which was *The Love of God and Spiritual Friendship* by Bernard of Clairvaux. While the works contained a wealth of truth, their sales fell short of the publisher's expectations, and today, they are no longer in print. We live in a shallow age, and literature such as is found in Classics of Faith and Devotion does not flourish in most modern bookstores. Yet the fact remains that these are time-tested classics. Now, I don't want to paint only a grim picture of our culture. There has been a kind of a reawakening and resurgence of interest in classic Christian writings in certain churches, seminaries, and universities. An example of this is the publication of a very helpful series called The Classics of Western Spirituality. One of the books in that series is *Bernard of Clairvaux: Selected Works,* and I will be referring to both of these editions in this chapter.

Despite some resurgence of interest in classic writings, I still fear that for most Christians there is little sense of the past. They simply jump from Martin Luther and John Calvin right to the present century with almost no knowledge of the first fifteen centuries of the church. What we need to notice as we look at this great literature is a hallmark of biblical focus and to see that it speaks to our own impatient and sensate culture.

Books like the one we are considering are meant to be read slowly, meditatively, and reflectively; we must not read them too quickly. In place of novelty, they focus on remembrance. They remind us of values that remain eternal. They teach us about living wisely and about being authentic. Some of them also remind us that life is not just a matter of *doing* but also of *being*.

James Houston, chancellor of Regent College, wrote a little section at the end of each Classics of Faith and Devotion text. It is simply called "A Guide to Devotional Reading," and in it he presents several principles of reading and reflection. Of these principles, the most important involves the selection of devotional reading materials. He urges that Christians not allow their enthusiasm for devotional literature to become a distraction from the priority of reading the Scriptures themselves as the primary source and resource. Devotional reading can be beneficial, but Scripture is foundational; it trains the heart. That is the difference between what we might call *informational* reading and *formational* reading. Informational reading involves more a search for questions and answers, but formational reading deals with the deepest issues of life, issues that remain relevant in any time period.

Houston also deals with the issue of pace. Many times we are in a hurry. We live in a hasty age where gratification has to be immediate. Yet we can assimilate things only so quickly, and devotional reading requires a deliberate pace. It demands regular, fixed reading times—an unhurried leisure. I think many people do not allow themselves the grace of personal margin in their lives, times when they can actually slow down enough to reflect on, digest, and explore scriptural truths.

It is also very important to be selective in our reading, for after all, every choice eliminates another; there is simply not enough time to read every worthy book. Therefore, we must choose wisely. There is wisdom in choosing from a broad spectrum of writers: Protestant, Catholic, and Orthodox, as well as ancient, medieval, and modern. There is a communion of saints that can be discovered in all periods of history. So, we don't want to let modernity make us parochial and limited to the biases of our own time.

There is a familiar quote by C. S. Lewis from the collection of his essays in *God in the Dock* where he says, "A new book is still on trial and the amateur is not in a position to judge it. The only safety is to have a standard of plain, central Christianity, which puts the controversies of the moment in their proper perspective. Such a standard can only be acquired from old books. It is a good rule, after reading a new book, never to allow yourself another new one until you have read an old one in between." Likewise, James Houston notes, "We tend to suffer from the literacy of too much rapid, superficial reading, or just mere glancing at books. Digestion, assimilation and then a lifetime of companionship with a book is a good test to see whether or not it is a classic of faith and devotion."

Keeping all that in mind, I want to begin by sharing some reasons why I have included Bernard of Clairvaux in this series. First, his corpus of writing is extensive. In fact, it would fill about 3,500 pages, but since he wrote on clay tablets, we have no original documents, manuscripts, or signatures of any sort. He lived from 1090 to 1153, and he was one of the most influential writers of the twelfth century. He was both contemplative and active, merging those two aspects of life well. He was part of the Cistercian monastic movement, more popularly known today as the Trappists. The Cistercian order advocated a more disciplined approach to Benedictine spirituality, named for an earlier, sixth-century monk.

Historically, Benedictine orders required monks to be obedient, to remain permanently with their monastery (leaving its walls only by permission of the abbot), and to commit themselves to worthy labor. During the Middle Ages, particularly in the years following the fall of Rome and the subsequent Teutonic invasions, Benedictine monasteries helped to reestablish order in a chaotic and decentralized Europe. They housed travelers, sent missionaries throughout Western Europe, pioneered and taught agricultural techniques, established schools for boys, kept vital historical records, and copied and preserved important writings that they stored in libraries within their monasteries. Much of what is known about that period of Western civilization is due to the diligence, scholarship, and preservation efforts of the Benedictines.

The Cistercian movement grew out of this earlier one, but as Benedictines had moved away from their strict roots, this newer order reemphasized a return to the more austere asceticism of the early Benedictine orders. Vows of silence were often part of a monk's devotion, for they believed that this permitted one to eliminate distractions and focus on one's relationship with God. There is certainly a value in exploring the practices and writings of these learned individuals, and many offer helpful insights into the Christian life. Yet a word of caution is needed here with regard to ascetic practices. God does not demand, nor is he pleased by, self-denial for the sake of self-denial, an error into which many people have fallen. There is a tendency sometimes to internalize spirituality and focus on one's own devotion as opposed to the external truth found in God's revealed Word and Christ.

While spiritual disciplines can be valuable servants, they make for oppressive taskmasters. There remains the danger that one may begin to place devotion and confidence in the vow or spiritual discipline, which is to lose focus on what Christ has done for us. For instance, in our hectic modern society, silence is rare. Developing the discipline to spend time with God and his Word in silence is necessary, yet the act itself must never become the emphasis. Disciplines properly applied improve our ability to study, hear, obey, and pray. Disciplines elevated to inappropriate places of honor ultimately promote an unhealthy self-focus and pride. Knowing and obeying God must remain the Christian's primary goals, and all that we do should serve to lead us to those two ends.

I am going to share with you some of my favorite highlights from Bernard's works. His writings were very Christ centered in emphasis, even though he espoused a decidedly mystical conception of the relationship between God and man and advocated a severe asceticism as necessary to the upward ascendance of the soul toward God and perfection. He defined the Christian life as a struggle between the elemental principles of the earth and this upward aspiration of the redeemed soul, asserting that the soul's true desire is the "embrace" of God. Here it is important to note that he, like many of the early church leaders—Augustine and Origen included—interpreted many passages of Scripture allegorically. This was the case with Bernard's interpretation of Song of Solomon. Whereas his predecessors had argued that the church universal was the manifestation of the bride symbol, Bernard interpreted the individual Christian's soul as the bride and, in so doing, promoted a quest for a sort of ecstatic union of the soul with Christ.

Bernard argued that this upward ascension of the soul toward a marriage union with Christ involved three stages: (1) repentance, (2) relationship, and (3) intimate union. In support of this view, he interpreted the Song of Solomon not as a treatise on human marriage but as a metaphor for the mystical marriage between the individual soul and Christ, believing that through ascetic discipline and purification such a state of spiritual ecstasy was possible, although admittedly, perhaps not in this life.

A problem with this hermeneutical approach to that book, though, is that the book itself is not presented as an allegory.

Rather, it appears to be a poetic and historical depiction of biblical love and marriage. For this reason, biblical scholars have taken varying positions on this portion of Scripture, as well as the lessons drawn from it. Yet a point on which most of us can agree is that life involves a upward journey of the soul as the Christian seeks to know and love God.

That is a major concept to keep in mind. We are constantly being pulled downward by the elementary principles of the earth. On the other hand, there is this desire of the heart to move from the flesh to the Spirit and to ascend on the wings of the Spirit to the heights for which we were created, namely, the embrace of God. I use that word *embrace* advisedly because Bernard was a real contemplative of the way of love. Love is a key theme in all his writings, and he continually returns to the idea of God's love for us, his provision of grace for us, and his desire for us to have an intimate fellowship with him. This is why he wrote eighty-six sermons on Song of Solomon and only got into the second chapter before he died. Imagine how many sermons he might have written had he lived longer! In those sermons, he interpreted that book on three allegorical levels: as a portrait of God's love for Israel, of his love for the church, and of his love for the individual soul. He asserted that in unity of love and singleness of fixed desire, it is possible for the body of believers to love properly, for we are all then attuned to the same One.

Do you see the idea? When two violins are tuned to a third, then they are also tuned to one another. This is why in an orchestra the entire orchestra tunes according to the note provided by the first violinist, for in that way they are all tuned to each other as well. So, that type of metaphor describes the basis, then, for his teachings on fellowship and genuine love.

The twelfth century was heavily influenced by love poetry, such as that of the troubadours in France. It was a whole genre of romance in a secular context; storytellers recounted the tragic love between legendary heroes such as Lancelot and Guinevere and Tristan and Isolde. But during this same time, there were writers who were also theologians, some of whom adapted these secular images of courtly love as spiritual metaphors. Bernard was one such writer/theologian. He wrote out of personal encounter and experience, relating with tremendous honesty his soul's struggle. That is why he remains relevant to us today; we all experience struggles of the soul, struggles between those things that are temporal and physical and those things that are eternal and invisible.

We find ourselves wanting better than what we often choose. We would like to know God better, we would like to pursue him more faithfully, but we find that there are so many things that pull us down: particular temptations, cultural distractions, habits, and people. With regard to these types of struggles, Bernard's writings have an enduring relevance, and I appreciate his tremendous honesty as well.

As I mentioned, love is the dominant theme of his writings and sermons. Bernard focused on love not merely in a personal way but as the basis of interpersonal and community experience. As we look deeply into the Word of God and beneath the surface, we find the story of a love and a lover—a story that can inflame a community of believers with the same passion. The Word then provides the basis for the personal and communal relationships because we are related by and being grounded in that same Word. The Word-centered approach makes personal and community relationships possible.

Bernard's message transcends the time and place of its writing. In describing his ego and personal life, he shares his own struggle. He lived and wrote at a time when the worth of an individual was beginning to be understood, a time that marked the first great synthesis in the West of scriptural and patristic theology on the one hand and the totality of human experience on the other. Bernard managed to reconcile personal and subjective experience with universal, objective teaching.

Bernard was born in 1090, and his family belonged to the minor nobility of Burgundy. His father was a knight, and his brothers were expected to become knights as well. We know very little about his youth, but Bernard later spoke vividly of his temptations with astonishing realism. It appears that he was an aggressive person, but he managed to control his aggression and keep it in check. In Bernard we have a man who was charismatic, energetic, intellectual, yet also passionate.

In 1111, at the age twenty-one, he decided to become a Cistercian monk, and his passion was so compelling that he managed to persuade his uncle, brothers, and a group of young noblemen, thirty-one individuals in all, to follow him into the same vocation. He even inspired his sister to become a nun.

In 1115 he was sent to found a monastery at Clairvaux, in the Champagne region of France. His brothers and friends all went with him at that time. Over a period of thirty-five years, he founded sixty-eight monasteries, becoming the principal promoter of the Cistercian order. By the time of his death, that order comprised some 350 houses, and about 160 of those were under his authority.

He exercised a tremendous influence on literally thousands of people through the ministries of the Cistercian order and through his writings. His first treatise was *On Steps of Humility and Pride*, which we will explore briefly, and then we will also look into his *Letter of Love* and his treatise entitled *On Loving God*. These writings have been merged in a compilation called *The Love of God*. He also wrote a key book *On Grace and Free Will*, borrowing one of Augustine's titles. His last work, a five-volume effort called *On Consideration*, was concerned with the whole issue of self-knowledge and the contemplation of God.

During his years of ministry, Bernard was also involved in a number of church disputes of that time period, and he traveled frequently both with and on behalf of the pope. He served as a member of the Knights Templar and even wrote a book *In Praise of the New Militia*. In fact, he preached in support of the Second Crusade—a French crusade—but that effort produced much suffering and regret. The crusade failed miserably, and Bernard was linked with its failure. This proved a painful episode in his life and in history.

Throughout his years of service, he eagerly sought clerical reform and wrote about that topic as well. Between his expansion of the Cistercian order, his political involvements, his reform efforts, and a personal ministry that included preaching and writing, Bernard significantly influenced his time period.

Throughout his life he was a man who sought to be God centered while remaining actively involved in the vital issues of his time. His death came in the summer of 1153, when he was sixty-three years old. Although he was worn out, he agreed to another trip, acting as a mediator for the pope. He died upon his return home in August 1153. Despite a relatively short life, he made much of the time he was given.

## Overview

One of the qualities I have come to admire in Bernard was his apparent ability to maintain a balance between a life of contemplation and a life of tremendous activity. That is a very hard balance to achieve, but he illustrates that it is possible to develop a contemplative dimension in one's life despite the demands of active service. I see this pattern beautifully illustrated in the life of our Lord, who often went away to quiet places to be with his Father. He carved out time to be alone with God. We must remember that there are no shortcuts to spiritual growth. Nothing can substitute for time spent with God.

Writing on this very topic, Bernard notes, "The writer achieves wisdom only with time." The problem today is that we tend to be in such a hurry and that we desire progress without much reading or study. Even our prayers are often hasty. In contrast, the ancient and medieval spiritual authors encouraged experience in a way that gave free rein to their imaginations. They used symbols and styles that might seem mysterious to us but that were designed to pierce the heart with desire and longing. Despite a heavy emphasis upon the experiential, Bernard also memorized huge amounts of

Scripture, as is obvious in reading his texts. Almost every other sentence seems to be some allusion to or some quotation from Scripture.

In his writings Bernard emphasizes the importance of becoming prepared to discern God's truth. He discusses the necessity of both humility and hope, something the medieval writers termed *compunction*. The promises of God's Word contrast the anxiety, loneliness, failures, and absurdity that often characterize life and offer an answer to reason's inability to explain everything. This medieval concept of compunction then involves two key components. In its stress of humility, it acknowledges the necessity of seeing ourselves and our human condition accurately. We are insufficient apart from God. We are depraved, alienated, and weak. But the other emphasis of compunction has to do with hope—not a vague hope, but the hope revealed in Scripture. God has intervened into our formerly hopeless situation, and he offers grace, redemption, and regeneration. He promises to empower us to act more consistently upon his will as we yield ourselves to him. So, knowing oneself becomes an important idea, but knowing God is far more significant. The awareness of the self leads to humility, but the grace of God provides us with a sense of hope.

With that in mind we will look through some of Bernard's writings. I want to mention two of his friends at this point because the friendships shed light on Bernard's own life and beliefs. William of St. Thierry and Ailred of Rievaulx were both longtime friends to Bernard, and both of them wrote on spiritual friendship. They considered friendship a sort of knitting together of souls that served to help one through the journey of life—spiritual traveling companions. There is not time enough to go into their writings in depth, but they have rich understandings that make some of our current ideas about friendship appear rather superficial. What we often call friendships these people would have termed only acquaintances at best, for they are not characterized by the openness, trust, and accountability of true friendship. These men understood that there is a kind of covenant that takes place in genuine friendship, where souls are knitted together for life in peace and in harmony and where there is a willingness to be brutally honest with one another. True friendship is willing to speak the truth and to love; true friendship is not afraid to be honest or to take the risks of rejection. Ironically, Bernard, William, and Ailred cultivated their friendship largely through correspondence, an art that has, for the most part, been lost today. A few moderns have prioritized correspondence, but not many. C. S. Lewis spent the first two hours of every day writing letters, and Thomas Merton spent about two hours a day writing letters as well. Huge volumes of these letters have recently been published.

Yet in general, our culture seems to be moving away from that. E-mails certainly aren't a substitute for thoughtful correspondence. I see them as a utility. If one wants to set an appointment, e-mail is a great tool; but if we want to communicate our hearts, it is not the way to go. There is just something much more meaningful about a letter that someone has taken the time and effort to write. Since friendship played a significant role in Bernard's spiritual development, it serves as a major theme in his writings and correspondence.

Many authors were influenced by Bernard's life and

writings, Dante among them. Dante incorporated Bernard as a character in his *Divine Comedy*. When Dante's protagonist self reaches the tenth sphere of heaven, he is met by Bernard. Expecting to see his previous guide, Beatrice, Dante explains, "I thought I should see Beatrice but I saw an old man, habited like the glorious people, overflowing was he in his eyes and cheeks with joys benign, an attitude of piety as to a tender father is becoming." This is his description of Bernard. Later, Bernard teaches Dante to look beyond Beatrice, even beyond the Virgin Mary, to the One beyond all others: "Bernard conveyed to me what I should do by sign and by smile. Already, on my own, I had looked up as he wished me to."

Clearly, Dante grasped Bernard's emphasis on divine love when he wrote, "Eternal light, that in thyself alone, dwelling alone, thus know thyself and smile on thyself love, so knowing and so known. My ruin and my desire were turned by love; the love that moves the sun and the other stars." That is how the whole *Divine Comedy* ends—with a picture of love. It is no surprise then that Dante chose Bernard for that significant role, for he was the theologian of love who explored the concept of love within the Trinitarian relationship; it was a major theme in his work.

Martin Luther was also inspired by Bernard's writings. He acknowledged that when Bernard preached on Christ, he had no equals among the church fathers. While Luther differed from Bernard in interpreting Scripture very literally rather than allegorically, he clearly held him in high regard in many areas of his life and teachings.

Bernard argued that man becomes most human when he becomes most godly and that godliness can develop only when he forgets himself and loves God. He wrote, "The less that we concentrate on self-development and the more we love Christ unabashedly, the more truly human we shall become." This is the idea that as we lose ourselves in the love of Christ, we become most truly who God created us to be.

This concept of the love of God became the theme of Bernard's life. In a poignant treatise on loving God he writes, "The righteous can claim no knowledge and no distinction for himself." He ascribes it all—and only—to God's own character, from whence all goodness is derived. He is quite firm on the grace of God. In his book *On Grace and Free Will*, he emphasizes grace by faith. He possessed a very clear grasp that one is not saved by a system of works. He then goes on to discuss this issue of loving God, saying, "It is not without fruitfulness or reward because the human heart cannot be satisfied by earthly things." He develops this very well, asking, "Who would ever dream of offering a reward to someone who longs and does so spontaneously?" Thus, for example, "no one will hire a hungry man to eat, or a thirsty man to drink or a mother to nurse her own child. Who could ever bribe a farmer to cultivate his own vineyard, or to dig around in his orchard or to rebuild his own house? How much more, then, that the soul that truly loves God asks for no other reward than to go on loving God. If the soul were to demand anything else then it would certainly love that thing and not love God."

He then alludes to the lack of contentment that people often experience: "Every natural person naturally desires to be always satisfied with what it esteems to be preferable. It is never satisfied with something which lacks the qualities it desires to have. So, if a man has chosen a wife because of her beauty then he will look out with a roving eye for more beautiful women. Or, if he is desirous of being well dressed he will look out for even more expensive clothes. No matter how rich he is, if wealth is his desire, he will envy those who are richer than he is." He continues by observing that "unsatisfied desires have no final satisfaction if they cannot be defined as actually the best or the highest. What makes men wonder, then, that a man who cannot find contentment with what is less or worse, since he seeks satisfaction in only what is highest and best? So, how stupid and mad is it to seek and find peace and satisfaction in that which cannot fulfill these needs? So, no matter how many things he may possess, he will always be looking for what is perceived to be still missing."

Here Bernard reminds us of the larger, eternal view. What we ultimately desire is something that only God can sustain and provide. The world cannot do this. He goes on to write, "This man prays continually for what is still lacking, with more anxiety in his preoccupation with what he lacks rather than have any joy or contentment in what he has already got." He continues, "In these ways then, the ungodly behave naturally, longing for whatever their desires immediately dictate. Like fools, they reject what would lead them to their true goal, which is not found in consumption but in consummation. They will wear themselves out in futility without reaching their blessed consummation because they stake their happiness on earthly things instead of upon their Creator. They seek to try, each one in turn, rather than to think of coming to Him, who is the Lord of the entire Universe."

Bernard developed a concept in his writings of what he termed *four degrees of love*. He argued that as the soul progresses through these stages of love, it moves away from inferior attachments. This particular treatise on love was probably written around 1125, and in it he asserts that in the first stage of human love "we love ourselves for our own sake. So man loves himself for his own sake. You have to start somewhere. Nature is so frail and weak that man is forced to love himself first of all." He is saying that this is necessary, but ultimately we have to begin to trust God to supply our needs rather than ourselves. We need God's love in order to be capable of going beyond ourselves—to love others in the truest sense of that word. Bernard states, "It is impossible to love *in* God without first *loving God*. God is the source of all goodness and is the source of our ability and disposition to love others. He has endowed us with the possibility to love. He who created our nature sustains them and protects them" (italics original).

He goes on to say, then, that the second stage, or degree, of love is when "man loves God for man's own blessing." In other words, he loves God, not for God's sake, but for his own sake. What he means by this is that man's love of God is still love for his own benefit, not for God's sake, yet by the grace of God, this type of love matures.

One then moves on, according to Bernard, to two final stages. In the third degree of love, he begins to love God for God's sake. This is a different kind of love, "where intimacy with God is the fruit of our need for God. Man's frequent need throws him back constantly upon God and through continual dependence he learns to enjoy God's presence." That is to say, God is willing to stoop to conquer. He is willing for us to come to him for all the wrong reasons. If he waited for us to come to him out of disinterested motives, or out of pious reasons, nobody would come to him. He knows this. Therefore he desires to pry open our fingers and loosen them from the things that we cling to so tightly. You know what that is like. You have to peel back one finger after another until finally you can release that false object and enjoy God himself.

Bernard asserts that these lesser stages of love provide a necessary transition to true love of God. In the fourth stage, however, man becomes forgetful of himself in light of his love of God. Bernard suggests that in that final stage, man finally understands his proper place within the created order. That is to say, we are no longer only ourselves, but we see ourselves as God's beloved. We see ourselves not as ourselves but as separate from ourselves. This is a very hard concept. Bernard further claims that "only the resurrected state can bring us to this level. Only when this has been relieved of these encumbrances will it be fully empowered by the grace of God. It is impossible to concentrate all love on God as long as the cares of this body keep one preoccupied to the point of distraction."

Likewise, I believe the command to love the Lord, our God, with all our heart, soul, and strength will not be fully possible until the heart no longer needs to think about the body. All of us can relate to this. We start to have a moment of intimacy and warmth with God, and then there are so many distractions that it disappears. Bernard goes on to assert, "It is only when the spiritual body is at peace and fully integrated as well as subjected to the Spirit in all things that the soul will hope to reach the fourth degree of love. Or rather it will be possessed by such love which only by the power of God can He establish us in such a condition."

Bernard grasps that such love cannot be obtained by human efforts. So, he really awaits the resurrected body when he says, "Body, soul and spirit, then will be made so complete that we will be absorbed in Him and we will enjoy this sense of genuine unity which can hardly be experienced in this life, but we can anticipate it with a great sense of joy and pleasure."

So this is the concept, then, that he develops in *The Love of God*, and it is radical in its nature. Listen to this prayer he wrote about loving Christ. It is from his twentieth sermon on the Song of Solomon: "Turn yourself, oh my God, toward me, so you will enable me to be humble. Take wholly to Yourself the brief remainder of the years that belong to my poor life, for all the years which I have lost because I have been preoccupied with losing myself, despise not, I entreat a humble and contrite heart. My days have declined as a shadow and they have perished without fruit." This prayer beautifully reflects the longing of this man's heart to know and love God properly.

As we discussed earlier, nearly everything in Bernard's writing is an allusion to one Scripture after another. This is the case when he writes, "You see that wisdom is the whole desire and purpose of my heart and if there is anything in me that is not employed in Your service, remove it. O God, You know my simplicity. If it is the beginning of wisdom in recognizing my ignorance, then I realize that this is Your gift. Increase it in me as I pray so that I will not be ungrateful for the least of Your benefits while I strive to supply that which is still lacking in me. It is, then, for these benefits that I love You with my feeble powers." He then goes on to discuss the idea of "learning to love Him tenderly, to love Him wisely, to love Him with a mighty love; tenderly so that you may not be enticed away from Him; wisely, so that you will not be deceived and so drawn away; and strongly so that you may not be separated from Him by any force."

The end of his treatise is on grace and free choice: "God, then, is the author of merit since He applied will to the good work and supplied the work to the will. If we wish to give significant names to our actions and to call them merits, it can only be in the seedbeds of our hopes, the incentives of love, the portents of a predestination, the harbingers of our future blessings, and the road to the divine kingdom. But there are no causes for pretending that we can rule like kings. In a word, we conclude as the apostle Paul began," and then he quotes from Romans 8:30: "These whom He predestined, He also called; and these whom He called, He also justified; and these whom He justified, He also glorified."

So you have a picture here of a man who has both a clear mind and a warm heart. His desire is, in the mistiness of the challenges and the fray of the daily temptations, to be a man of fidelity, hope, and purpose, a man who strives to know the very love and character of the living God. Bernard's writings reveal a man whose soul is inflamed, and they speak to us with the sense of vibrancy and liveliness of a man who is humbly honest about his own emotions and his own struggles. The key to humility, may I say, is not being aware of how sinful we are. The key to humility is becoming increasingly aware of the grace and goodness of God, so much so that we no longer focus on ourselves but are amazed at the fact that all of life is a gift of grace. The more we come to understand God's offer of grace, the less circumstances can disturb our tranquility and our repose.

We will tend to forget that daily, yet we want to continually recover our sense of gratitude as we seek to know God. Humility involves a real sense of being enraptured with God. It also includes an experiential apprehension. This is something C. S. Lewis touched on in *Mere Christianity* when he noted, "It is after you have realized that there is a real Moral Law, and a Power behind the law, and that you have broken that law and put yourself wrong with that Power—it is after all this, and not a moment sooner, that Christianity begins to talk. When you know you are sick, you will listen to the doctor. When you have realized that our position is nearly desperate you will begin to understand . . . how God Himself becomes a man to save man from the disapproval of God." Once again, we see that humility grows out of both desperation and hope. Yet the despair is overcome by the grace of God and the hope revealed in Scripture.

In light of that truth, perhaps one of most moving quotations from Bernard's writing is found in his summary on the stages of love. There he exhorts us to "admit that God deserves to be loved very much, yea, boundlessly, because He loved us first, He infinite and we nothing, loved us, miserable sinners, with a love so great and so free. That is why I said at the beginning that the measure of our love to God is to love immeasurably. For since our love is toward God, who is infinite and immeasurable, how can we bound or limit the love we owe Him? Besides, our love is not a gift, but a debt."

Father, we ask that we would be lovers of you. We pray that you would give us the grace of holy desire and that we would pursue you above every other good, treasuring the things that you deem to be important and investing enough time to seek solitude and true devotion, where we can reflect deeply on who you are, in the mystery of your grace and in light of who you have made us to be. As we discover who you are more and more, may we find ourselves. We pray in Christ's name. Amen.

# NOTES

# Also Available

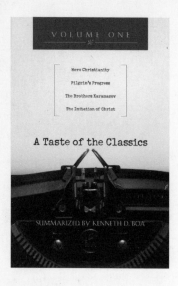

Engage more of Dr. Boa's insights into our rich heritage of Christian literature. See these other volumes:

**Volume One**
- Mere Christianity
- Pilgrim's Progress
- The Bothers Karamazov
- The Imitation of Christ

**Volume Two**
- The Screwtape Letters
- Paradise Lost
- Confessions of Augustine
- The Pursuit of God

**Volume Three**
- Crime and Punishment
- Pensées
- The Great Divorce
- Christian Perfection

**Volume Four**
- The Divine Comedy
- The Knowledge of the Holy
- Pride and Prejudice
- The Love of God

**Retail: $9.99**
**Volume One ISBN: 978-1-93406-810-6**
**Volume Two ISBN: 978-1-93406-811-3**
**Volume Three ISBN: 978-1-93406-812-0**
**Volume Four ISBN: 978-1-93406-813-7**

**Available for purchase at book retailers everywhere.**